This Book

is the exclusive property of

M _____

of _____

_____

He that will have a cake
out of wheat must needs
tarry at the grinding.

—*Shakespeare.*

A B∞k
For A Cook

BEING A SELECTION OF CERTAIN RECIPES
AND OTHER THINGS WHICH EVERY
GOOD HOUSEKEEPER KNOWS BUT
IS APT TO FORGET. ALSO CER-
TAIN RECIPES AND OTHER
THINGS WHICH ARE NEW
AND HERE FOR THE
FIRST TIME
PUBLISHED

FACSIMILE EDITION

1994

APPLEWOOD BOOKS
Bedford, Massachusetts

A *Book for a Cook* was first published by Pillsbury in 1905.

Copyright © 1905 by L. P. Hubbard.
© The Pillsbury Co.

When A *Book for a Cook* was first published in 1905, tastes and health standards concerning the preparation of food were very different than they are today. Please note that for the sake of history this book has been reissued as it was first published and there has been no attempt to retest and update each recipe. Statements about eggs on page 45 and the use of raw eggs in recipes on pages 58, 64, and 113 have been retained for historical reasons. Raw eggs are now considered a possible source of salmonella and should not be used in the preparation of any recipe.

ISBN: 1-55709-225-7

Thank you for purchasing an Applewood Book. Applewood reprints America's lively classics—books from the past that are still of interest to readers today. For a free copy of our current catalog please write to: Applewood Books, 18 North Road, Bedford, MA 01730.

10 9 8 7 6 5 4 3 2

Library of Congress Cataloging in Publication Data
A Book for a cook: being a selection of certain recipes and other things...–Facsimile ed.
      p.   cm.
  Originally published: Minneapolis: Pillsbury, 1905.
  Includes index.
  ISBN 1-55709-225-7
  1. Cookery, American.
TX715.B7226   1994
641.59'73 – dc20   94 –1089
                             CIP

A Book
For A Cook.

BEING A SELECTION OF CERTAIN RECIPES
AND OTHER THINGS WHICH EVERY
GOOD HOUSEKEEPER KNOWS BUT
IS APT TO FORGET. ALSO CER-
TAIN RECIPES AND OTHER
THINGS WHICH ARE NEW
AND HERE FOR THE
FIRST TIME
PUBLISHED

PILLSBURY

MINNEAPOLIS, MINNESOTA

MAISON MACHIN FRÈRES

AUGUSTE MACHIN

90. Rue de Turenne

PARIS

253-94

Paris, le *190*

St. Louis, Dec. 5th, 1904.

Mr. Henry L. Little,
    Manager the Pillsbury Flour Mills,
    Minneapolis, Minn.

Dear Sir:-

    Permit me to congratulate your firm
on the very high honor given to your
Exhibit and Pillsbury's Best.

    Your flour is very good, rich in
fine gluten so necessary to good bread
and pastry.

    We have used your Pillsbury's Best
exclusively at our Parisian World's Fair
Bakery with great satisfaction.

    Your brand is well known to us in
Paris. We have also been honored with
a grand prize for general excellence.

      Very truly yours,

        MACHIN FRERES.

    Machin Brothers are proprietors of forty bakeries
in Paris, France, supplying the hotels with their
French bread and fancy pastry and cakes.

·INTRODUCTION·

"The way to a man's heart is thru his stomach."

THE makers of PILLSBURY'S BEST have studied the practical needs of bread-makers. They have from time to time published recipes and other suggestions which have been appreciated by the American home-makers.

It was not however until the World's Fair of 1904 at St. Louis that the contents of this book were complied for them by Mrs. Nellie Duling Gans, who there demonstrated her superiority as a baker and a cook by making the bread that took the Grand Prize, the highest award possible, using PILLSBURY'S BEST flour, and secured for her personally the Medal of Honor for "Perfect Bread."

Herewith is presented some of her well-tried and popular recipes. They are not offered as a general cook-book, nor as a guide for experts, but simply as a help to the average housekeeper, in the hope that they will make easier her search after variety without calling too much upon her means.

Pillsbury's Household
Correspondence Department.

THE failure or incomplete success of a recipe oftentimes depends upon some little detail that has been misunderstood or overlooked in the preparation. Although the following recipes have been thoroughly tested, and we know them to be absolutely correct, yet to any user of this book who has failed to obtain satisfactory results, or who is in need of still more explicit directions, we will gladly furnish the services of an expert woman as a correspondent, who will answer all questions and give any suggestions possible.

In writing, please note carefully the following directions:

1.—Address all communications to DEPARTMENT C., PILLSBURY, MINNEAPOLIS.

2.—Inclose a stamp for reply.

3.—Write your name and address in the upper left hand corner of your letter.

4.—Name the recipe or recipes for which you wish help, and tell fully the character of the result you obtained.

_____

NOTE:—We cannot be responsible for recipes, if other flour than PILLSBURY'S BEST is used.

·CONTENTS·

CONTENTS--Cont.

CONTENTS—Cont.

WHAT IS YEAST?

Yeast is a microscopic plant of fungus growth, a collection of living one-celled organisms that partakes of the nature of plant life.

How does it Grow?

With proper warmth, moisture and food, the walls of these little one-celled plants bulge on the side in an oval shape. This bulge soon separates from the parent cell and becomes an independent organism. Other cells form in the same way from the parent cell, and also from each new cell, and thus the yeast plant multiplies.

What of its Care?

The little yeast cells are tenacious of life, and can live under most adverse circumstances. They are killed by exposure to heat above the boiling point of water, but they endure cold much better, being able to continue life in a suspended form at two degrees below freezing. From 65 to 72 degrees Fahrenheit is most favorable to the growth of yeast. The best collection of yeast cells massed together in a dormant state, is the ordinary yeast cake, either dry or compressed.

How long does it Live?

Yeast cells may be kept alive and vigorous for many days if kept in a dry and cool place.

What is its Relation to Flour and Bread?

The yeast is softened in water to separate the yeast cells that they may be easily distributed through the flour.

In the starch and gluten of the flour, they find their food. Sugar hastens their growth, while salt retards it.

The yeast cells, finding their favorite food, begin to grow, changing the starch of the flour into sugar, and the sugar into carbonic gas and alcohol. The gas, in its efforts to escape, expands the elastic gluten of the dough in which it is mixed, and lifting up the mixture, the bread is "raised."

By subjecting the dough to heat (baking), the alcohol and carbonic gas are driven out and the cell-walls are fixed, and thus sweet bread is produced.

For reasons stated above, your flour and utensils should always be warm.

The life of the yeast is constantly in jeopardy, while age to flour, if properly kept in a dry place, improves its quality.

BREAD

"A whole train a quarter of a mile in length, known as a Flour Flyer, leaves the milling district every day, bound for some big Eastern city, where it is distributed by Eastern buyers, and this is only a part of the flour that is shipped. Sometimes a great shipment goes to Europe; sometimes to South Africa; again to Japan, the Phillipines, even Australia."

—*A Kernel's Story.*

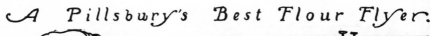

"He who has no bread has no authority."

"With bread all griefs are less."

BREAD.

Good bread is the great need in poor homes, and oftentimes the best appreciated luxury in the homes of the very rich.

Compared with wheat flour, all other bread materials are insignificant.

Of all the important foods, wheat bread contains the most nutrition. Bread made from Pillsbury's Best Flour is richer in good nourishment than any other food article that the world has produced.

The recipes here presented for bread are those which earned for the author the highest award at the World's Fair of 1904 in St. Lous, and they are presented with especial and complete confidence in their practical value to the housekeeper.

LIGHTNING BREAD.

Materials:

1 tablespoonful salt.
3 tablespoonfuls flour.
7 medium sized potatoes.

2 tablespoonfuls sugar.
1 pint boiling water.

Way of Preparing:
Yeast:

Stir salt, flour, sugar and hot water well together. Then add the potatoes boiled and mashed fine, one pint of the hot water in which they were boiled and three pints cold water, then stir in two and one-half cakes of yeast previously dissolved in a little lukewarm water, cover with a cloth and keep warm ten hours. Then put it in a moderately cool place for use as needed.

Bread:

For each loaf of bread put four cups of sifted, warm flour, a cupful of scalded milk and a tablespoonful of lard in the bread pan. Stir the yeast, take one pint of it and mix with the flour into a soft dough, using a large spoon. Then knead it briskly ten minutes, mold into loaves and let rise once in a warm place. When light bake forty-five minutes.

BAKING POWDER BISCUITS.

Materials:

2 cups Pillsbury's Best.
2 teaspoonfuls baking powder.
1 teaspoonful salt.
1 cup milk and water (half each).
1 tablespoonful butter.
1 tablespoonful lard.

Way of Preparing:

Sift the flour, salt and baking powder together twice. Cream butter and lard together, and add it to the dry ingredients, using the tips of your fingers. Then add the liquid, mixing with a knife, until you have a very soft dough. Place on your mixing board. Pat out lightly until three-fourths of an inch thick. Cut out and bake in a hot oven for fifteen minutes.

Quantity:

This will make two dozen biscuits.

BAKING POWDER DOUGHNUTS.

Materials:

1 cup sugar.
2 eggs.
2 tablespoonfuls butter.
2 teaspoonfuls baking powder.
2 cups Pillsbury's Best.
1 cup milk.
1 teaspoonful salt.
½ teaspoonful nutmeg.

Way of Preparing:

Cream the butter and sugar, add the eggs, well-beaten, and then the milk.

Sift the flour, salt, baking powder and nutmeg together and add them.

Roll out one-half inch thick, cut out with a doughnut cutter and fry in deep fat.

When they are cool, sprinkle with powdered sugar.

Quantity:

This recipe makes two dozen doughnuts.

BEATEN BISCUITS.

Materials:

1 lb. Pillsbury's Best.
1 teaspoonful salt.
2 oz. lard.
A pinch of soda.
Sweet milk.

Way of Preparing:

Sift the flour, salt and soda. Then work in the lard. Then use enough sweet milk to make a very stiff dough.

13

Beat for twenty minutes until the dough blisters. Roll out about three-fourths of an inch thick, cut out and prick each biscuit once with a fork, place in biscuit pans, and bake in a moderate oven twenty minutes.

Quantity:

This will make four dozen small biscuits.

EGG BISCUITS.

Materials:

2 cups Pillsbury's Best.	½ cup milk.
2 teaspoonfuls baking powder.	1 tablespoonful butter.
	1 tablespoonful lard.
1 teaspoonful salt.	1 tablespoonful sugar.
	Whites of 2 eggs.

Way of Preparing:

Sift flour, baking powder, salt and sugar together twice. Cream butter and lard together and add it to the dry ingredients, using the tips of your fingers. Then add the milk mixed with the whites of the eggs, mixing with a knife until you have a very soft dough. Place on your molding board. Pat out lightly until three-fourths of an inch thick. Cut out and bake in a hot oven fifteen minutes.

Quantity:

This will make 24 biscuits.

BOSTON BROWN BREAD.

Materials:

2 cups cornmeal.	1 pint hot water.
2 cups entire wheat flour.	1 cup molasses.
	½ cake of yeast.
1 teaspoonful salt.	½ cup lukewarm water.
1 teaspoonful soda.	

Way of Preparing:

Scald the cornmeal with the pint of hot water, then mix in the two cups of entire wheat flour, the molasses and the salt, adding the yeast dissolved in ¼ cup of lukewarm water. Lastly add the soda, also dissolve in ¼ cup of lukewarm water. Pour this batter into greased molds, filling each a little over half, and let them rise until they are nearly full.

Then put the molds into a pot of rapidly boiling water. Boil three hours, take them out and bake them for half an hour.

Quantity:

This will make two large loaves.

Note:—In boiling let the water come up to the molds two-thirds of their height, and when it boils away add more boiling water.

14

BREAD AND POTATO BREAD.

Materials:

1 pint milk.	2 tablespoonfuls butter.
1 cup water.	1 tablespoonful sugar.
9 cups Pillsbury's Best.	1 teaspoonful salt.
1 cake of yeast.	¼ cup lukewarm water.

Way of Preparing:

Scald the milk and one cup of water, and while scalding hot pour the liquid over the butter, sugar and salt. Dissolve the yeast in ¼ cup of lukewarm water.

When the milk has cooled to lukewarm, beat into it four cups of flour and add the dissolved yeast. Mix thoroughly, cover and set to rise. When it is light and frothy add to it the other five cups of flour, until the dough ceases to stick to your hands and to the board. The quantity of flour to be added may be more or less than five cups; the moisture in the flour determines that: when the dough ceases to stick you have added enough.

Now knead the dough for about fifteen minutes and then set it to rise until it obtains twice its size, when you form it into loaves and place them into baking pans.

Let them rise again until they reach double their size, place them into an oven and bake forty-five minutes.

Quantity:

This will make three loaves in bread pans of ordinary size. To make the old-fashioned potato bread, add to the sponge of the above recipe two medium-sized white potatoes, boiled and mashed while warm.

CHOCOLATE DOUGHNUTS.

Materials:

2 eggs.	2 tablespoonfuls melted chocolate.
1 tablespoonful melted butter.	1 teaspoonful vanilla.
1 cup sweet milk.	3 cups Pillsbury's Best.
¾ cup sugar.	2 teaspoonfuls baking powder.
½ teaspoonful salt.	

Way of Preparing:

Sift together the flour, baking powder and salt. Beat the eggs and add to them the sugar, chocolate, butter and milk. Then add the vanilla.

15

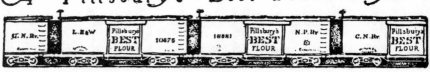

Now add the sifted ingredients, making a medium dough. Roll out one-half inch thick, cut out
with a doughnut cutter and fry in hot fat. When
cool sprinkle with powdered sugar.

Quantity:

This will give three dozen doughnuts.

CORN BREAD.

Materials:

2 cups yellow cornmeal	2 cups Pillsbury's Best.
2 teaspoonfuls baking powder.	1 teaspoonful salt.
	1 pint milk.
3 eggs.	½ cup boiling water.
2 tablespoonfuls melted butter.	

Way of Preparing:

Pour the boiling water over the cornmeal, and
let it get cool; sift the flour together with the baking powder and salt. Beat the yolks of the eggs
until they are light, then add them to the cornmeal
and then add the milk, the flour and the melted
butter; beat to a smooth batter and beat the whites
of the eggs to a stiff froth.

Add the latter to your mixture, stirring it in
quickly.

Pour all into a shallow, well-greased pan and
bake in a hot oven twenty-five minutes.

Quantity:

Enough to serve six persons.

CORNMEAL MUFFINS.

Materials:

1 cup cornmeal.	1 cup sour milk.
1 cup Pillsbury's Best.	2 eggs.
1 teaspoonful soda.	2 tablespoonfuls melted butter.
1 teaspoonful salt.	
¼ cup molasses.	

Way of Preparing:

Sift together the cornmeal, flour and salt. Dissolve the soda in the sour milk, and then add it to
the sifted ingredients.

Then add the molasses and beat thoroughly.
Add the eggs, well-beaten, and lastly the melted
butter. Bake in hot, well-greased pans, in a moderately hot oven half an hour.

Quantity:

This will give twelve muffins.

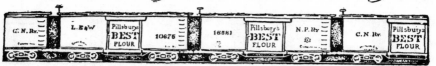

CRESCENTS.

Materials:

1 quart warm water.	2 tablespoonfuls sugar.
1 yeast cake.	Sifted flour.
1 tablespoonful salt.	

Way of Preparing:

Mix the sugar, salt, yeast and water. When thoroughly dissolved, add enough sifted flour to make a medium soft dough. Cover, keep in a warm place, and let rise until light, then turn it onto the kneading board. Knead thoroughly and roll out into a sheet one-half an inch thick. Now cut in 6-inch squares, then divide them diagonally, so you will have triangular pieces, brush these lightly with water and roll them up, beginning on the longest side of each. Place into a buttered pan, bringing the two ends around towards each other into crescent shape. Let rise until light, brush with egg and water, and bake in a moderately hot oven fifteen to twenty minutes.

DELICATE CORN BREAD.

Materials:

1 cup yellow cornmeal.	2 eggs.
1 cup Pillsbury's Best.	1 tablespoonful melted
1 teaspoonful baking	butter.
powder.	½ teaspoonful salt.
1 pint milk.	1 cup of milk.

Way of Preparing:

Sift the yellow cornmeal and the flour. Beat the yolks of the eggs and add them to the pint of milk, then add the melted butter.

Add to the meal and flour the salt and baking powder. Then make a smooth batter with the other ingredients. Lastly stir in the stiffly beaten whites of the eggs. Thoroughly butter a bread-pan, and pour in your batter, which should be two inches deep. Finally pour into the middle of the pan one cup of sweet milk, taking care to do it gently, and not to stir.

Place in a moderate oven and bake forty-five minutes. Remove from the oven, cut into squares, with a hot knife and serve at once.

The center will have a custard-like appearance.

Quantity:

Sufficient to serve six persons.

DOUGHNUTS.

Materials:

2 cups Pillsbury's Best.
½ teaspoonful salt.
½ tablespoonful butter.
½ cup sour milk.
¾ teaspoonful soda.

1 teaspoonful **cream of tartar.**
¾ cup sugar.
1 egg.
½ teaspoonful nutmeg.

Way of Preparing:

Sift flour with the salt, sugar, cream of tartar, soda and nutmeg. Beat the egg and add to it the milk. Work the butter into the sifted ingredients and then add the milk and egg. Roll out one-half inch thick, cut out with a doughnut cutter and fry in deep fat.

When cool sprinkle with powdered sugar.

Quantity:

This will make two and one-half dozen doughnuts.

GRAHAM BREAD.

Materials:

4 cups graham flour.
3½ cups Pillsbury's Best.
2 tablespoonfuls molasses.
3 cups lukewarm milk.
1 cake yeast.

1 heaping teaspoonful salt.
2 tablespoonfuls brown sugar.
½ teaspoonful soda.
2 tablespoonfuls butter.
½ cup lukewarm water.

Way of Preparing:

Sift together the graham flour, wheat flour, brown sugar and salt, then rub in the butter. Add the molasses with the soda dissolved in it. Next add the lukewarm milk and lastly the yeast dissolved in the lukewarm water.

Knead the dough well for twenty minutes and set it to rise covered up. After rising form it into two loaves, put them into pans and let them rise again.

Graham bread requires longer to rise than white flour bread. Bake in a moderately hot oven for an hour and a quarter.

If graham bread is baked too quickly it is apt to become doughy in the center.

Quantity:

The above makes two loaves of bread.

EASY ENTIRE WHEAT BREAD.

Materials:

1 quart entire wheat flour.	¼ cake yeast.
3 tablespoonfuls sugar.	2 tablespoonfuls warm water.
1 teaspoonful salt.	

Way of Preparing:

Sift the flour, sugar and salt. Mix with enough warm water to make a batter, as stiff as it can be stirred. Dissolve the yeast in two tablespoonfuls of warm water, then add it to the batter. Beat for ten minutes. Let rise over night. In the morning beat again. Put in greased pans. Let rise again. Bake in a moderate oven one hour.

Quantity:

This will make one large or two small loaves.

KUGELHUPF.

Materials:

1 cup butter.	4 cups Pillsbury's Best.
¾ cup sugar.	1 cup milk.
7 eggs.	1 teaspoonful salt.
1 cake yeast.	1 cup seeded raisins.
1 teaspoonful vanilla.	2 oz. shredded almonds.

Way of Preparing:

Scald the milk and let it cool. Then make a sponge of the flour, salt and ¾ cup of the milk. Beat ten minutes and add the yeast previously dissolved in the other ¼ cup of the milk. Let stand until light.

Soften the butter, add the sugar and three of the eggs. Then add this mixture to the sponge. Mix thoroughly and add the remaining eggs one at a time. Then add the vanilla and raisins. Butter two Turk's-head molds and sprinkle with shredded almonds.

Half fill them with the mixture and let them stand until they are full. Bake fifty minutes. Turn from molds and cover with powdered sugar.

Quantity:

This makes two loaves.

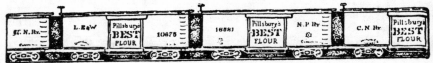
LEMON BUNS.

Materials:

½ cup sugar.
2 tablespoonfuls butter.
2 cups milk.
1 cup currants.
¼ cup lukewarm water.
6 cups Pillsbury's Best.

2 eggs.
1 cake yeast.
½ teaspoonful salt.
1 lemon.
¼ teaspoonful nutmeg.

Way of Preparing:

Cream the butter and sugar, then add the eggs well beaten. Mix thoroughly and add two cups of flour, then the milk, which must be just lukewarm, then the other four cups of flour. Lastly add the yeast dissolved in the warm water. Beat for fifteen minutes, cover closely and let it rise. When risen, stir in the currants, which must be floured, then add the nutmeg, the grated rind and half the juice of a lemon.

Place on your pastry board, roll out half an inch thick and cut out with a medium-sized biscuit cutter.

Place half the buns in greased biscuit pans, leaving plenty of space.

Then place the other half on top of those already in the pans, making them in pairs. Let rise until very light and bake in a quick oven. After they are done brush the top of each with the white of an egg and sprinkle with powdered sugar.

Quantity:

Three dozen.

LOVERS' KNOTS.

Materials:

1 cup scalded milk.
2 tablespoonfuls sugar.
½ teaspoonful salt.
½ yeast cake, dissolved in 4 tablespoonfuls of lukewarm water.

2 tablespoonfuls melted butter.
1 egg.
Grated rind of one-half lemon.
Pillsbury's Best.

Way of Preparing:

Add sugar and salt to the milk. When lukewarm add the dissolved yeast and 1½ cups of flour. Cover and let rise. When light add the well-beaten egg, lemon rind and butter; then enough flour to knead; let rise again. Roll out in a sheet one-half inch thick, cut into strips ½ inch wide and 9 inches long, take up each strip and tie into a knot. Place in a buttered pan, allowing some space between each two, let rise until light and bake in a hot oven from fifteen to eighteen minutes.

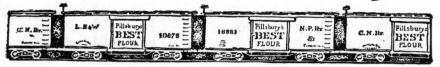

MUFFINS No. 1.

Materials:

2 tablespoonfuls butter. 1 pint milk.
2 tablespoonfuls sugar. 2½ cups Pillsbury's Best.
2 eggs. 2 teaspoonfuls baking
½ teaspoonful salt.   powder.

Way of Preparing:

Cream the butter and sugar and add the beaten yolks of the eggs. Sift the flour, baking powder and salt and mix with the former, alternating with the milk. Lastly add the stiffly beaten, whites of the eggs.

Have your gem pans hot and well greased, and bake in a hot oven twenty minutes.

Quantity:

This will make eighteen muffins.

MUFFINS No. 2.

Materials:

1-3 cup butter. 4 teaspoonfuls baking
¼ cup sugar.   powder.
¼ teaspoonful salt. 1 egg.
  ¾ cup milk.
  2 cups sifted flour.

Way of Preparing:

Cream butter and sugar; add the well-beaten egg. Mix the flour, salt and baking powder and stir in gradually, adding the milk gradually also. Beat thoroughly, turn into hot, greased muffin pans, and bake 25 minutes.

Quantity:

Will make twelve muffins.

NUT BREAD.

Materials:

2 cups milk. 1 teaspoonful salt.
2 cups water. 1 cup chopped nuts.
1 tablespoonful lard. ½ cup lukewarm water.
4 cups Pillsbury's Best. 5 cups whole wheat
1 cake yeast.   flour.
2 tablespoonfuls sugar.

Way of Preparing:

Scald milk and water together, and pour them over the sugar, salt and lard. Let cool until medium hot, then add the white flour. Beat ten minutes and then add the yeast, dissolved in the one-half cup lukewarm water. Cover and let rise until very light. Then add the nuts and the whole wheat flour making a soft sticky dough. Place the dough in a buttered bowl and let it rise until it gains twice its original bulk. Then form into loaves.

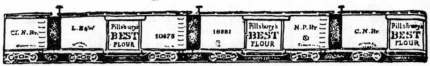

Place them into pans, having each half full, let them rise until the pans are full; then bake them for one hour.

Quantity:

This amount makes three loaves.

PARKER HOUSE ROLLS.

Materials:

3 tablespoonfuls butter.	1 pint milk.
1 teaspoonful salt.	1 tablespoonful sugar.
½ cup lukewarm water.	1 cake yeast.
6 cups sifted flour.	

Way of Preparing:

Scald the milk and pour it over the sugar, salt and butter. Allow it to cool, and when it is luke-warm, add the yeast, dissolved in the lukewarm water, and then add three cups of flour. Beat hard, cover and let rise until it is a frothy mass. Then add three more cups of flour. Let it rise again until it is twice its original bulk, then place it on your kneading board. Knead lightly and then roll it out one-half an inch thick.

Take a biscuit cutter and cut out the rolls. Brush each piece with butter, fold and press the edges together, and place them in a greased pan, one inch apart. Let them rise until very light. Bake in a hot oven fifteen minutes.

Quantity:

This recipe makes three dozen Parker House rolls.

POPOVERS.

Materials:

2 cups Pillsbury's Best.	2 cups milk.
3 eggs.	1 teaspoonful salt.

Way of Preparing:

Beat the eggs until very light. Add the milk and salt and pour gradually into the flour, beating all the time.

Beat the batter very smooth and strain through a sieve. Have your gem pans lightly greased, and very hot. Quickly fill half full of the batter. Place in a hot oven and bake twenty-five minutes. They should feel dry to the touch.

Quantity:

This will make eighteen popovers.

POTATO BREAD.

(See previous pages for bread and potato bread.)

SALT RISING BREAD.

Materials for the Yeast:

1 pint hot water.
1 teaspoonful salt.
1 heaping tablespoonful
  white cornmeal.

11 heaping tablespoon-
  fuls sifted flour.

Materials for the Bread:

10 cups Pillsbury's Best.
1 heaping tablespoonful
  lard.

1 pint warm milk.
½ teaspoonful salt.

Way of Preparing the Yeast:

Cool the water sufficiently to bear your finger in it, then add the salt, cornmeal and lastly ten tablespoonfuls of flour. Beat until smooth, then sprinkle the remaining tablespoonful of flour over the top of the mixture. Cover and let stand in a warm place five hours. By that time the clear water should have risen on top of the mixture. Drain off this water and beat the mixture thoroughly. Set aside for another hour, at the end of which time the mixture should have become light and frothy. It is now ready for use.

Way of Preparing the Bread:

Sift your flour into your mixing bowl, add the salt, and with the tips of your fingers work in the lard. Now make a well in the center of the flour, pour in your yeast preparation and then the milk. With a spoon begin to stir and continue until it is too stiff to admit of further using the spoon. Turn it out on the molding board, knead until smooth, divide into four parts and place them in buttered baking pans, having each pan half full. Let rise until they are full. Bake forty-five minutes.

Quantity:

This will make four loaves in an ordinary sized bread pan.

SWEET POTATO BISCUITS.

Materials:

2 cups Pillsbury's Best.
1 cup buttermilk.
1 tablespoonful sugar.
½ teaspoonful soda.

1 cup mashed sweet po-
  tatoes.
1 teaspoonful salt.
1 tablespoonful butter.

Way of Preparing:

Mash the boiled sweet potatoes smooth, add the sugar and then the butter. Dissolve the soda in the buttermilk and add it. Sift flour and salt and add them to the other mixture. Roll out, cut as other biscuits, and bake in a quick oven.

Quantity:

This will make twenty-four biscuits.

SWEET RUSKS.

Materials:

2 tablespoonfuls sugar.	2 eggs.
2 tablespoonfuls butter.	½ teaspoonful salt.
1 cup milk.	4 cups Pillsbury's Best.
½ cake yeast.	¼ cup warm water.

Way of Preparing:

Cream the butter and sugar, then add the well-beaten yolks of the eggs and then the stiffly beaten whites. Sift in the flour and salt and add the milk gradually. Add the yeast dissolved in the warm water.

Cover and let it rise. When very light, pour it into a buttered biscuit pan, filling it half full. Let it rise until the pan is quite full.

Bake in a moderate oven for thirty minutes. When done cut in long narrow strips.

Quantity:

The above will make rusks for six persons.

TEA ROLLS.

Materials:

2 cups milk.	1 teaspoonful salt.
3 tablespoonfuls butter.	6 cups Pillsbury's Best.
2 eggs.	¼ cup lukewarm water.
1 cake yeast.	1 teaspoonful ground
½ cup sugar.	cinnamon.

Way of Preparing:

Scald the milk, and pour it over the sugar, butter and salt. When it has cooled to lukewarm, beat into it three cups of flour, sifted three times. Then add the yeast, dissolved in the lukewarm water, Cover and let it rise until it is a frothy mass. Then add the eggs, well-beaten, the flour and the cinnamon.

Place in a buttered bowl. Let is rise until it has twice its original size. Form it then into small rolls, place them into a buttered pan, and let them rise until very light. Brush the tops with melted butter and bake in a hot oven for fifteen minutes.

Quantity:

This will make four dozen rolls.

COCOA ROLLS.

Cocoa rolls are made by adding to the above one-half a cup of ground cocoa.

VIENNA ROLLS.

Materials:

Same as those used for "Crescents."

Way of Preparing:

The difference in preparing Vienna rolls and Crescents consists in the rolling and shaping.

When the dough is prepared, ready for molding, shape the same as small Vienna loaves about six inches long. Place in a buttered pan, allowing a little space between each two, and let them rise. When light, gash the tops diagonally three times; bake in a moderate oven about twenty-five minutes. If desired you may brush the rolls with beaten eggs and sprinkle them with poppy-seeds, in which case you omit gashing them.

WAFFLES.

Materials:

2 cups Pillsbury's Best.
1½ cups milk.
1 tablespoonful sugar.
½ teaspoonful salt.
2 eggs.
1 tablespoonful melted butter.
2 teaspoonfuls baking powder.
Honey.

Way of Preparing:

Sift the flour, baking powder, salt and sugar, add the milk and the well-beaten yolks of the eggs. Then add the butter and lastly the stiffly beaten whites of the eggs. Fry on a very hot, well-greased waffle iron and serve immediately with fresh honey, maple syrup, jelly or molasses.

Quantity:

The above will make two dozen waffles.

WHITE CORN BREAD.

Materials:

2 eggs.
½ cup Pillsbury's Best.
1 cup milk.
2 teaspoonfuls baking powder.
1 heaping cup white cornmeal.
2 tablespoonfuls butter.
1 teaspoonful salt.
½ cup boiling water.

Way of Preparing:

Beat the eggs without separating whites and yolks, add the milk to the eggs. Sift the flour, salt and baking powder together. Pour the boiling water over the cornmeal and let it cool, then add the flour, salt and baking powder, sifted, and then the milk and eggs. Lastly add the butter, after melting it. Bake in a hot oven for twenty-five minutes.

Quantity:

Sufficient to serve five persons.

CAKES

Dost thou think because thou art virtuous,
there shall be no more cakes?—Twelfth Night.

Cake-making requires more judgment than any other department of cooking. Nevertheless it is the one most frequently tried by the beginner.

There are two classes of cakes; those with butter and those without it. The former embraces pound, cup and fruit cake. To the latter belong sponge, sunshine and angel-cake.

Always mix your cake in an earthen bowl. The baking of cake requires more care than the mixing. Divide your baking time into quarters; during the first it should begin to rise, during the second it should finish rising and begin to brown, in the third it should continue to brown and during the fourth and last it should finish browning and leave the sides of the pan. Bake your cake with nothing else in the oven and keep it as near the oven center as possible. Remove the cake from the pan as soon as it leaves the oven, and place it on a sieve or a napkin covered board.

ALMOND TARTS.

Materials:

4 eggs.
1 cup powdered sugar.
½ cup chocolate, grated.
1 teaspoonful baking powder.
½ lb. almonds, blanched and chopped fine.
1 cup cracker dust.
Whipped cream.
Candied fruit.

Way of Preparing:

Beat the yolks of the eggs until very thick, add the sugar gradually, and then the stiffly beaten whites of the eggs. Then add the cracker dust, chocolate, almond and baking powder. Bake in gem pans. When cold remove the centers and fill with whipped cream. Garnish with candied fruit.

Quantity: This will make eight tarts.

ANGEL FOOD.

Materials:

1 cup of egg whites, unbeaten.
1¼ cups of sugar.
Pinch of salt.
1 cup sifted Pillsbury's Best.
1 teaspoonful cream of tartar.
1 teaspoonful almond flavoring.

Way of Preparing:

Put a pinch of salt into your egg whites and beat until frothy. Put in the cream of tartar and finish beating. Then beat in the sugar. Add the flavoring and fold in the flour lightly. Bake in an ungreased pan with a tube in a moderate oven for half an hour.

Sift the sugar once, the flour five times, and have the eggs very cold.

Quantity:

This makes one large cake.

CHOCOLATE COOKIES.

Materials:

1 square bitter chocolate.	¼ cup milk.
	2 eggs.
2 teaspoonfuls baking powder.	½ cup butter.
	1 cup sugar.
Pinch salt.	2½ cups Pillsbury's Best.

Way of Preparing:

Cream the butter and sugar, add the well-beaten eggs, and then the chocolate, melted, sift the flour, salt and baking powder together and add alternating with the milk. Then roll out, cut with small fancy cutter and bake in a moderate oven.

Quantity:

This will make four dozen cookies.

CREAM PUFFS.

Materials:

1 cup Pillsbury's Best.	¼ lb. butter.
¾ cup water.	5 eggs.
Pinch of salt.	Filling.

Way of Preparing:

Heat the water and add the butter and salt. when this mixture boils stir in the flour; take care to have no lumps. Cook until the mixture leaves the sides of the saucepan. Pour out into another pan, and allow it to cool. When nearly cold add the unbeaten eggs, one at a time. Mix in each one thoroughly before adding the next. When all the eggs have been added, cover the mixture and let it stand for one hour. When ready to bake drop it by the spoonful on buttered tins, leaving space for them to rise. Bake in a moderate oven, for forty-five minutes. They should then feel dry and crisp to the touch. When cold split and fill with whipped cream, custard or jam. If desired they may be fried in deep fat the same as doughnuts. If you intend frying them drop only teaspoonfuls instead of tablespoonfuls at a time into the fat.

Quantity:

This will make eighteen baked.

DEVIL'S FOOD.

Materials:

¼ cup chocolate.
½ cup sugar.
½ cup milk.
1 egg.
2 teaspoonfuls vanilla.
1 cup sugar.

½ cup butter.
1 egg and 1 yolk.
1 cup milk.
1 teaspoonful soda.
2 cups Pillsbury's Best.

Way of Preparing:

Put the one-half cup of milk in a double boiler. Melt the chocolate and add to it one-half a cup of sugar, and one egg well beaten. When the milk is boiling hot add it. Put back into the boiler and cook five minutes. Remove and let it cool. Cream together one cup of sugar and half a cup of butter, add one egg and the yolk of another and beat for five minutes. Then add the cup of milk with the soda dissolved in it, and then the flour. Lastly add the vanilla and combine the two mixtures. Mix thoroughly and bake in layers. Put together with chocolate filling.

Quantity:

This makes one medium-sized cake.

LEMON COOKIES.

Materials:

½ cup butter.
1 cup sugar.
2 eggs.
2 tablespoonfuls milk.

2 teaspoonfuls baking powder.
3 cups Pillsbury's Best.
1 teaspoonful lemon extract.

Way of Preparing:

Cream the butter, add the sugar, the eggs well beaten, milk and lemon. Sift the dry ingredients and add them to the mixture. Chill and roll out thin, using half the dough at a time. Cut in fancy shapes and bake in a moderate oven.

Quantity:

This will make five dozen cookies.

LEMON GEMS.

Materials:

½ cup sugar.
2 eggs.
½ cup butter.
Pinch salt.
1 cup Pillsbury's Best.

1 teaspoonful baking powder.
Grated rind and juice of one lemon.

Way of Preparing:

Cream the butter and add the sugar. Add the well-beaten yolks of the eggs and the lemon rind. Sift together the flour, salt and baking powder and add them. Then add the lemon juice and lastly the stiffly-beaten whites of the eggs.

Bake in gem pans in a moderate oven.

Quantity:

This will make eight gems.

LORENA CAKE.

Materials:

1¼ cups sugar.
½ cup butter.
2 eggs.
2 cups Pillsbury's Best.
2 teaspoonfuls baking powder.
1 teaspoonful almond extract.
¾ cup milk.
1 pint whipped cream.
1 square chocolate.
½ cup boiling water.
1 tablespoonful cornstarch.
Grated rind and strained juice of 1 orange.

Way of Preparing:

Beat the eggs and add one cup of sugar, then the butter creamed, one-half cup of milk and the baking powder and flour sifted together, add the grated rind and strained juice of one orange, and bake in a border mold. When cool, but not cold, fill in the center with the whipped cream, piling it up. Then pour around the cake a hot sauce made by cooking one cup of sugar, cornstarch, boiling water, one-fourth cup of milk and chocolate in a double boiler until they have the consistency of thick cream. Flavor with the almond extract. Serve hot.

Quantity:

This will serve eight persons.

NUT COOKIES.

Materials:

1-3 cup butter.
½ cup sugar.
2 eggs.
½ cup Pillsbury's Best.
1 teaspoonful baking powder.
¾ cup chopped nuts.
1 teaspoonful lemon juice.

Way of Preparing:

Cream the butter and add the sugar and eggs well beaten. Sift the flour and baking powder together. Add the first mixture. Then add the milk, nuts and lemon juice. Drop from a spoon on an unbuttered baking sheet, leaving an inch space between them. Sprinkle with chopped nuts and bake in a very slow oven.

Quantity:

This will make two dozen cookies.

POUND CAKE.

Materials:

1 lb. butter.
1 lb. sugar.
1 lb. Pillsbury's Best.
12 eggs, using yolks of 9.
2 tablespoonfuls rosewater.
½ cup sherry wine.

Plowing in "the land of Pillsbury's Best".

Way of Preparing:

Cream the butter, gradually adding the sugar, and beat ten minutes. Beat the yolks of 9 eggs until very thick and lemon colored. Then gradually add them to the butter and sugar and beat again. Sift the flour three times and add it slowly, beating all the time. After adding the flour beat for fifteen minutes. Then add the rosewater and sherry and beat again. Lastly, add the stiffly-beaten whites of the eggs. Fold them in, and bake immediately. Use a pan with a tube in the center and bake in a moderate oven for an hour and a half.

Quantity:

This will make one large cake or two medium-sized ones.

PLAIN CAKE.

Materials:

½ cup butter.	1 teaspoonful soda.
1 cup sugar.	1 cup raisins.
2 eggs.	2½ cups flour.
1 cup sour milk.	1 teaspoonful cinnamon
	½ teaspoonful cloves.

Way of Preparing:

Cream butter and sugar; add well-beaten eggs. Dissolve soda in two teaspoonfuls of cold water, and beat it into the sour milk. Combine the mixtures, add spices and flour gradually. Cut raisins and add. Bake forty-five minutes in a slow oven.

Quantity:

This mixture makes one loaf.

SOFT GINGER BREAD.

Materials:

¾ cup molasses.	3 cups Pillsbury's Best.
1 cup brown sugar	1 tablespoonful ginger.
½ cup butter.	1 teaspoonful cinnamon
1 cup sour milk.	1 teaspoonful soda.
3 eggs.	

Way of Preparing:

Cream the butter and sugar, and add the molasses. Then add the eggs, one at a time, and beat thoroughly.

Melt the soda in the sour milk, mixing well. Sift the flour and spices and add to the other mixture, alternating with the milk. Bake either in gem pans or in a ginger cake tin.

Quantity:

This will make twenty-four gems or one large cake.

STRAWBERRY SHORTCAKE.

Materials:

4 teaspoonfuls baking powder.	⅞ cup milk. Flour.
½ teaspoonful salt.	2 cups Pillsbury's Best.
2 tablespoonfuls sugar.	Strawberries, 1 quart.
¼ cup butter.	

Way of Preparing:

Mix flour, baking powder, salt and sugar and sift twice. Work in butter with fingers. Add milk gradually. Put on board, divide into two parts, and roll out to fit the cake tin: using the least possible flour to roll. Put one part on tin, spread lightly with melted butter, then place other part on top. Bake fifteen minutes in hot oven. When baked, the two parts will separate easily without cutting. Mash berries slightly, sweeten and place between cakes. A dozen or so whole berries may be placed on top for a decoration.

Quantity:

Will cut into eight pieces.

SUCCESS CAKE.

Materials:

2 cups sifted Pillsbury's Best.	3 level teaspoonfuls baking powder.
1½ cups confectioners' XXXX sugar.	1 teaspoonful flavoring extract.
½ cup butter.	½ cup water.
Whites of five eggs.	

Way of Preparing:

Cream the butter and sugar and add the water. Never mind its looks. Then add the flour and baking powder, after sifting them mixed together. Stir this thoroughly and then add the stiffly-beaten whites of the eggs. After that beat it for five minutes. Finally add the flavoring extract, whichever one you prefer and bake immediately.

Quantity:

This will make either a loaf cake or a layer cake.

THREE MINUTE CAKE.

Materials:

2 eggs.	½ teaspoonful cinnamon
½ cup milk.	½ teaspoonful grated nutmeg.
1 1-3 cups brown sugar.	
1-3 cup butter.	½ lb. stoned dates, cut in pieces.
1¾ cups Pillsbury's Best.	
3 teaspoonfuls baking powder.	

Way of Preparing:

Put all the ingredients together in a bowl and beat them for three minutes. Then bake them in a cake-pan for from thirty-five to forty minutes. Be sure to put all ingredients in together; adding them separately will cause failure.

Quantity:

This will make one medium-sized cake.

Harrowing in "the Land of Pillsbury's Best."

WHITE FRUIT CAKE.

Materials:

1 lb. Pillsbury's Best.
1 lb. sugar.
Whites of 16 eggs.
¾ lb. butter.
2 teaspoonfuls baking
powder.
Rind of one lemon.
1 cocoanut, grated.

1 lb. almonds, blanched
and shredded.
1 lb. citron, cut fine.
1 lb. candied lemon
peel, minced.
2 tablespoonfuls rose-
water.
2 tablespoonfuls sherry
wine.

Way of Preparing:

Cream the butter and sugar, add the rosewater
and sherry and then the baking powder and flour
sifted together.

Beat the whites of the eggs very stiff and fold
in. Lastly add the grated cocoanut and other ingredients. Bake for three hours in a slow oven.
Use a deep pan with a tube in the center.

Quantity:

This will make one large or two small cakes.

CAKE FILLINGS AND FROSTINGS.

BOILED ICINGS.

Materials:

2 cups sugar.
¼ cup water.

Stiffly beaten whites of
two eggs.

Way of Preparing:

Boil the sugar and water until it forms a thick
syrup. Then gradually pour it into the beaten eggs,
beating the mixture rapidly all the time. When all
in, and the mixture has thickened and is cool, it is
ready for use in icing cakes.

CARAMEL FILLING.

Materials:

1 lb. brown sugar.
½ cup milk.

2 eggs.
Vanilla.

Way of Preparing:

Boil the sugar and milk until it will harden when
dropped into cold water. Beat the yolks of the
eggs and the whites separately and then combine
them. Gradually pour over them the hot syrup,
beating all the time. Add the flavoring and beat
until cool and quite thick.

CHOCOLATE FILLING.

Materials:

1 cup sugar.
¼ cup Pillsbury's Best.
2 eggs.
2 cups milk.

1 teaspoonful vanilla.
2 squares chocolate.
1 pinch salt.

Way of Preparing:

Heat the milk in a double boiler, mix the dry ingredients and the eggs lightly beaten. Gradually add the hot milk. Return to the boiler and cook fifteen minutes. Melt the chocolate and add it. Cool and flavor.

FONDANT ICINGS.

Materials:

1 lb. sugar.
½ cup water.
XXXX Confectioners' sugar.

1 tablespoonful boiling water.
Flavoring extract.

Way of Preparing:

Boil the sugar and water until the syrup will spin a heavy thread when dropped into cold water. Carefully pour the syrup out on a large platter. When cool enough to bear your finger in it stir the mixture rapidly until it is soft, white and creamy. Dust your bread board with XXXX sugar, turn the mixture on it, and knead it as you would biscuit dough, until it is very soft and smooth. Let it cool, place in your double boiler and melt, stirring all the time. Add one tablespoonful of boiling water, flavor to taste and pour over your cake while hot.

MAPLE SUGAR FILLING.

Materials:

½ cup maple sugar, grated.

½ cup sweet milk.
Whites of two eggs.

Way of Preparing:

Put the sugar into an agate saucepan and add the milk. Boil it until it will spin a thread. Have the whites of the eggs beaten very stiff and add the syrup gradually, beating all the time. When it begins to get quite thick place it quickly between the layers of the cake.

ORANGE FILLING.

Materials:

2 oranges.
½ cup water.

2 cups sugar.
2 egg yolks.
½ lemon.

Way of Preparing:

Grate the yellow rind from the peel of the oranges. Put the water in a saucepan and add the grated orange peel. Boil five minutes and strain. Add enough hot water to make one-half a cup. Now add the water to the two cups of sugar and boil until it spins a thread. Pour it then over the well-beaten yolks of the eggs and beat until cool. Add the juice of half an orange and the juice of the half lemon.

CANDY

Sweets to the Sweet.

—Hamlet.

CANDIED ORANGE PEEL.

Materials:

1 cup water.   1 cup sugar
2 cups peel of orange.   Dry sugar.

Way of Preparing:

Cut the peel in long strips and measure two cups of them. Put them in a sauce pan and pour the water over them. Cook until tender. Drain off the water and add the sugar. Gradually heat and when the sugar is melted cook over a slow fire, until the peel is clear. Remove from the fire and when cool dip in dry granulated sugar and pack in jars.

CANDY PUFFS.

Materials:

1 lb. sugar.   1 cup chopped nuts.
1 cup water.   1 teaspoonful flavoring
Whites of 2 eggs.   extract.

Way of Preparing:

Boil the sugar and water until they form a heavy thread. Beat the whites of the eggs very stiff. Pour the syrup slowly over the beaten eggs, stirring all the time. When all the syrup has been used, keep beating until the mass begins to harden, then add the flavoring and nuts, mix thoroughly and place by the spoonful on a greased platter. Make the puffs the size and shape of a large egg.

COCOANUT KISSES.

Materials:

1 fresh cocoanut, grated   Whites of 2 eggs.
½ its weight in pow-   ½ teaspoonful flavoring
    dered sugar.   extract.

Way of Preparing:

Grate the cocoanut and weigh it, add the sugar, mixing well. Beat the whites of the eggs very stiff, and add them to the grated cocoanut and sugar. Beat the mass hard for five minutes. Add the flavoring extract, then drop it in small spoonfuls on buttered paper, and dry in a slow oven for fifteen minutes.

Quantity:

This will make two dozen kisses.

FONDANT.

Materials:

1 lb sugar.
XXXX sugar.

½ cup water.

Way of Preparing:

Boil the sugar until the syrup will spin a heavy thread when dropped into cold water. Carefully pour it out on a large platter. When cool enough to bear your finger in it, stir the mixture rapidly until it is soft, white and creamy. Dust your bread board with XXXX sugar, turn the mixture on it, and knead it as you would biscuit-dough until it is very soft and smooth. It is now ready for use.

Fondant is the basis of all cream candy.

ICE CREAM CANDY.

Materials:

4 cups granulated sugar
½ cup water.
1 teaspoonful cream of tartar.
½ cup vinegar.

1 tablespoonful glycerine.
1 teaspoonful flavoring extract.

Way of Preparing:

Boil the sugar, water, vinegar and glycerine together, until the mixture will spin a heavy thread. Remove from the fire and when it no longer boils add the cream of tartar and flavoring extract. Pour on a large buttered platter, and when sufficiently cool pull until white.

Quantity:

This will make two pounds.

MAPLE PUFFS.

Materials:

½ lb. maple sugar.
½ lb. brown sugar.
Whites of 2 eggs.
1 cup English walnuts.

½ cup chopped figs.
½ cup chopped citron.
½ cup raisins.
½ cup water.

Way of Preparing:

Boil the sugar and water until they spin a heavy thread. Beat the whites of the eggs very stiff, gradually add the hot syrup to the whites of the eggs, beating all the time. When the mixture begins to stiffen, add the other ingredients. Beat until it will hold its shape.

Place by tablespoonfuls on greased paper and let stand until stiff.

Quantity:

This will make twelve puffs.

Seeding in "the Land of Pillsbury's Best".

CEREALS

ABOUT CEREALS.

Grains in some form or other are used as breakfast dishes. The principal ones are wheat, rye, corn, rice, oats and barley.

Oatmeal is perhaps the best known among the products of these grains. Rye meal, cornmeal, hominy, (which is also a corn,) are derived from them. These and others may be boiled or cooked in a double boiler by steaming, with a plentiful supply of water in the boiler, and while the grains should be allowed to swell to their full extent, it is recommended not to have the mush too soft, which would cause it to be swallowed without allowing the teeth to operate.

It takes about six hours to cook whole oatmeal; hominy four hours; Indian or cornmeal from three to six hours; rice from 25 to 35 minutes, according to the grade of rice; cracked wheat two hours.

In cooking cereals from packages it will be found that the cooking time, as a rule, exceeds that mentioned in the directions.

In cooking cereals the following general rule may be observed.

Put a teaspoonful of salt in a quart of water to boil directly over the fire and stir in a cup of the cereal and when this boils, when all the cereal has been stirred in, set over heated water and keep on cooking, without stirring, the time required by experience.

Raisins and sweet fruits may be added in flavoring cereals.

Harvesting in "the land of Pillsbury's Best."

36

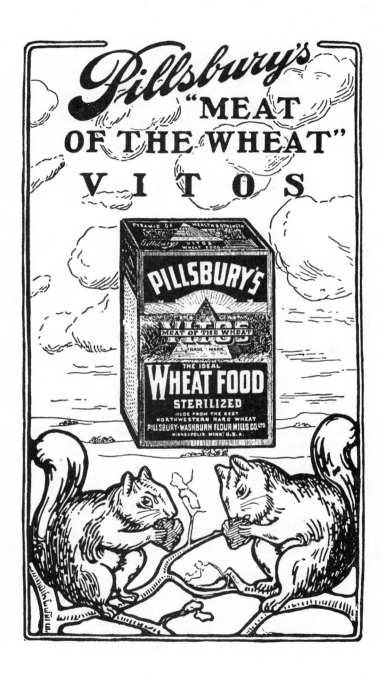

A DAINTY BREAKFAST DISH.

Materials:

1 cup Pillsbury's Vitos. Salt to taste.
4 cups boiling water. Cream.
                           Sugar.

Way of Preparing:

Stir the Vitos into the boiling water, salt to taste, and boil 15 minutes. Serve with cream and sugar.

Best results are obtained by using the double boiler.

FRIED VITOS MUSH.

When the Vitos as in above recipe is cold, slice it, dip into beaten egg and fry.

Serve with syrup.

BOSTON BROWN BREAD.

Materials:

2¼ cups sour milk. 1 teaspoonful salt.
½ cup molasses. 1½ level teaspoonfuls
2 cups Pillsbury's Vitos soda.
1 cup Pillsbury's Best.

Way of Preparing:

Mix the sour milk, molasses, Vitos, flour and salt; add the soda, dissolved in one tablespoonful of warm water.

Beat thoroughly, turn into a well-buttered mold and steam four hours.

IDEAL BREAKFAST BREAD.

Materials:

2 eggs. 1 cup Pillsbury's Vitos.
1 tablespoonful sugar. 1 cup Pillsbury's Best.
2 cups milk. 1 teaspoonful salt.
3 level teaspoonfuls
   baking powder.

Way of Preparing:

Beat the eggs, add the sugar and the milk. Then mix the Vitos, flour, salt and baking powder.

Add first mixture gradually to second mixture, to make a smooth batter. Pour into a well-buttered frying pan. Take one cup milk and pour here and there over the mixture; then bake in a hot oven.

38

VITOS SPICED CHOCOLATE CAKE.

Materials:

½ cup butter.
1½ cups fine granulated sugar.
Yolks of 3 eggs, well beaten.
Whites of 3 eggs, beaten until stiff.
2 squares Baker's chocolate, melted.
1½ cups Pillsbury's Best.
4 level tablespoonfuls baking powder.

1 teaspoonful allspice.
1 teaspoonful cinnamon
½ teaspoonful cloves.
1 cup Pillsbury's Vitos.
½ cup milk.
½ cup water.
Beaten whites of 2 eggs.
½ teaspoonful vanilla.
1½ cups sugar boiled for icing.

Way of Preparing:

Cream the half cup of butter, add gradually the granulated sugar, the yolks and whites of the three eggs and the chocolate.

Then mix and sift the flour, baking powder, allspice, cinnamon and clove, and add the Vitos.

Add to this the first mixture alternately with one-half cup of milk. Bake in layer cake pans and spread between and on top vanilla icing made thus:

Boil 1½ cups sugar with ½ cup water until syrup will thread when dropped from the tip of the spoon. Pour slowly onto the beaten whites of two eggs, and beat until of consistency to spread. Flavor with ½ teaspoonful of vanilla.

PILLSBURY'S VITOS COFFEE.

Materials:

1 cup Pillsbury's Vitos.
The white of one egg.
5 cups boiling water.

Scalded milk or cream.
Cut sugar.

Way of Preparing:

Put the Vitos into an iron frying pan, set on top of the range and roast slowly, stirring frequently until the Vitos is of an even golden-brown color. Store in a glass jar. Scald a granite-ware coffee-pot that has never been used for ordinary coffee. Moisten ½ cup cereal coffee with the white of the egg.

Turn into coffee pot, and add five cups boiling water.

Let boil thirty minutes, let stand on the back of the range five minutes to settle.

Serve with scalded milk or cream and cut sugar.

Much cheaper than any cereal coffee on the market.

VEAL CROQUETTES.

Materials:

2 cups finely chopped cooked veal.
Salt, pepper and celery salt.
1 cup Pillsbury's Vitos mush.
Crumbs and beaten eggs.

Cream sauce made by melting 2 level tablespoonfuls butter, adding 2 level tablespoonfuls flour, and pouring on gradually two-thirds cup of cream.

Way of Preparing:

Mix the chopped veal with the mush, which should be made stiff by using two parts of boiling water to one part of Vitos.

Season highly with salt, pepper and celery salt.

Chill, shape it in cones, dip in egg, crumbs and egg again and fry in deep fat. Serve with tomato or cream sauce.

VITOS GEMS.

Materials:

1 cup Pillsbury's Best.
Maple syrup.
4 level teaspoonfuls baking powder.
½ teaspoonful salt.
½ cup Pillsbury's Vitos.
2 tablespoonfuls melted butter.
1 cup milk.

Way of Preparing:

Mix and sift the flour, salt and baking powder, then add the Vitos. Beat the yolks of the eggs, add the milk, and combine the mixtures; then add the melted butter and the whites of the eggs, beaten until stiff.

Turn into hot, buttered gem pans and bake in a hot oven twenty-five minutes. Serve with maple syrup.

FRUIT CEREAL.

Materials:

2 cups water boiled with ½ teaspoonful salt.
White of one egg, beaten stiff.
½ cup Pillsbury's Vitos.
1½ cups berries, strawberries or raspberries preferred.
5 tablespoonfuls cream.
Whipped cream.

Way of Preparing:

Add gradually to the salted boiling water the half cup of Vitos. Let boil two minutes, then cook in double boiler 30 minutes. Add the cream and cook two minutes. Remove from fire and add the white of one egg, beaten stiff, and the berries.

Pour into moulds, first dipped in cold water, chill and serve with whipped cream, sweetened and flavored. When berries are out of season the Vitos may be molded in individual molds with a teaspoonful of jelly in the bottom of each.

VITOS GRIDDLE CAKES.

Materials:

4 eggs.
4 tablespoonfuls melted butter.
3 level teaspoonfuls baking powder.

2 cups milk.
2 cups Pillsbury's Vitos mush.
Pillsbury's Best.

Way of Preparing:

Beat the yolks of the eggs until light, add the milk, butter, mush, baking powder, and enough flour to make a stiff batter.

Cut and fold in the whites of four eggs, beaten until stiff. Cook on a hot, well-greased griddle, and serve with maple syrup.

STEAMED VITOS PUDDING.

Materials:

2 cups scalded milk.
1 cup Pillsbury's Vitos.
½ cup molasses.
2 well beaten eggs.
2 tablespoonfuls melted butter.

1 teaspoonful soda.
1 teaspoonful salt.
1 cup seeded raisins (or dates).

For Sauce:

¼ cup butter.
1 cup sugar.
Yolks of two eggs.

Grated rind of 1 lemon.
Juice of 2 lemons.

Way of Preparing:

Add gradually to the scalded milk, stirring constantly, the one cup of Vitos. As soon as the mixture thickens, remove from fire and add the molasses, the two beaten eggs, the melted butter, soda, salt and raisins. Dates may be used in place of raisins. Turn into a buttered pudding mould and steam for three hours.

Serve with lemon sauce made thus:

Mix ¼ cup butter, one cup sugar, the yolks of two eggs, and the lemon juice and rind.

Cook on top of double boiler until the mixture thickens, stirring occasionally.

This furnishes a delicious, inexpensive dessert for eight.

WITH A CHAFING-DISH

The chief pleasure in eating does not consist in costly seasoning, or exquisite flavor, but in yourself.
—Horace.

The use of the chafing dish is, contrary to general opinion, far older than our present civilization. It reaches, in some form back into the times of the ancient Greeks and Romans.

As used at present, alcohol is the fuel for the lamp attached to it, and a tray is desirable to protect tablecloths and tables from alcohol and fire. The cap covering the opening through which the lamp is filled should be kept in place after filling it. Otherwise, controlling the flame is hardly possible. It is, of course, also possible to connect for heating purposes, with gas and electricity.

Chafing-dish cooking is not done by the average housekeeper.

A chafing-dish needs to be watched carefully from a chair with a high seat to make its use comfortable. For the benefit of the comparatively few, who can and care to indulge in its use, the following recipes are presented.

CREAMED DISHES.

Materials for the Cream:

1 cup milk.	1 tablespoonful butter.
1 cup cream.	½ teaspoonful white
1 teaspoonful salt.	pepper.
1 tablespoonful flour.	8 drops onion juice.

Way of Preparing:

Mix cream and milk and bring them to the boiling point. Cream flour and butter together and add to them the salt, pepper and onion juice. Now combine the two mixtures and cook until they have the consistency of thick cream. Remove from the fire. It is ready for use.

Creamed oysters, shrimps, lobster, fish, chicken, turkey, lamb, tongue, dried beef, peas, cauliflower, etc., are made by adding the cooked fish, meat or vegetable to the above cream sauce and the flavor may be varied by adding chopped parsley, celery, salt, curry-powder or lemon juice.

Sweetbreads are particularly good when served in this manner.

OMELETTE.

Materials:

4 eggs.
2 yolks.
Grated rind one orange.
¼ teaspoonful salt.
2 large oranges, sliced.
4 tablespoonfuls orange juice.

1 tablespoonful water.
3 tablespoonfuls powdered sugar.
1 tablespoonful butter.
½ cup powdered sugar.

Way of Preparing:

Beat the yolks of all the eggs until thick; add the sugar, salt, orange juice, and grated rind. Melt the butter in your chafing dish, fold the stiffly-beaten whites of the eggs into the yolk-mixture. When the butter is melted and hot turn the omelette into the dish and cook over the hot water for fifteen minutes. Remove and hold the blazer directly over the flame until the omelette is slightly brown. Extinguish the lamp and serve the omelette directly from the blazer.

When serving, garnish the omelette with the sliced orange and dust with the powdered sugar.

Quantity:

This will serve four people.

OYSTER STEW.

Materials:

1 cup milk.
½ cup cream.
½ teaspoonful salt.
2 dozen oysters.

1 heaping tablespoonful butter.
¼ teaspoonful pepper.
¼ cup cracker crumbs.

Way of Preparing:

Melt the butter in the chafing-dish and add the milk, cream and seasonings. When boiling hot add the oysters. Cook them until they look plump. Add the cracker crumbs and serve.

Quantity:

This will serve four persons.

PEACH SANDWICHES.

Materials:

1 stale sponge cake.
1 can of peaches.
2 tablespoonfuls butter.
½ cup sherry wine.
½ cup sugar.

½ teaspoonful powdered cinnamon.
Grated rind one orange.
1 pint whipped cream.

Way of Preparing:

Slice the sponge cake into one-half inch slices. Stamp out with a fancy cutter twice as many round pieces as you have persons to serve. Melt the butter in your chafing dish and brown in it the pieces of cut-out sponge cake. Remove them to a platter, drain the peaches, having as many halves of peaches as you have pieces of sponge cake. To the butter in your chafing dish add the sugar, sherry and grated orange peel. When these ingredients are hot add the drained peaches. Cook five minutes. Extinguish the lamp and prepare to serve. When serving place on a small plate one round of sponge cake, on this place one-half a peach, on top of this peach place another round of sponge cake and put another half peach on top of the latter. Dust with a pinch of cinnamon and garnish with whipped cream.

Quantity:

Serve one sandwich to each person.

TAPIOCA AND GRAPE JUICE PUDDING.

Materials:

1 cup grape juice.	Pinch of salt.
1 cup water.	Stiffly beaten whites of
1 cup sugar.	three eggs.
¼ cup minute tapioca.	Cream.
Juice of two lemons.	

Way of Preparing:

Soak the tapioca for fifteen minutes in the cup of water. Place in a chafing dish and add the sugar. When hot add the grape juice. Cook until the tapioca is transparent. Then add the lemon juice and salt. Lastly fold in the beaten whites of the eggs.

Serve either hot or cold with plain cream.

Quantity:

This will serve six persons.

WELSH RAREBIT.

Materials:

1 tablespoonful butter.	½ cup ale.
1 egg.	⅛ teaspoonful salt.
⅛ teaspoonful pepper.	5 slices toast, toasted
¼ teaspoonful soda.	on one side only.
½ lb. cheese.	

Way of Preparing:

Melt the butter in your chafing dish and then add the cheese broken into small pieces; stir without stopping until the cheese is melted. Add the egg, beaten and diluted with the ale, lastly add the salt, pepper and soda.

Serve immediately on the toast with the untoasted side up.

Cream may be substituted for the ale if desired.

Quantity:

This will serve five people.

EGG DISHES

"Oh eggs within thine oval shell,
What palate tickling joys do dwell."

It takes no Christopher Columbus to discover that—

Eggs have two advantages over all other foods. First, they are procurable nearly everywhere; second, the most dainty person is sure when eating eggs that they have not been handled. They possess their highest nourishing value in their raw state, and the longer an egg is subject to heat the harder it is to digest.

Eggs are digested more readily when the whites and yolks are thoroughly mixed before cooking, therefore in a scrambled state and as omelettes they are the easiest digested. Eggs are at their very best when only twelve hours old. A fresh egg feels heavy and sinks flatly to the bottom in water. They may be kept for months by packing them small ends down in ordinary coarse salt. Each should stand upright and not touch another.

EGG CROQUETTES.

Materials:

¼ cup butter.
½ cup Pillsbury's Best.
1 egg.
¼ teaspoonful pepper.
1 tablespoonful chopped parsley.
*½ cup white stock.
½ cup cream.
½ teaspoonful salt.
8 hard boiled eggs.
1 teaspoonful onion juice.
1 pint parboiled oysters.

Way of Preparing:

Make a sauce with the butter, flour, cream, stock, uncooked egg, well-beaten, the salt and pepper. Then add to it the cooked whites of eggs, chopped fine and the yolks passed through a vegetable press. Lastly add the chopped parsley and the onion juice. Let this mixture get cold, then form into egg-shaped croquettes with an oyster in the center of each. Now egg, crumb and fry them in deep fat. Garnish with parsley when serving.

Quantity:

This will serve six.

*"White Stock" will be found under "Soups."

45

EGGS WITH CREAM DRESSING.

Materials:

2 tablespoonfuls butter.	1 teaspoonful salt.
3 tablespoonfuls flour.	Few grains pepper.
1½ cups milk.	3 hard boiled eggs.

Way of Preparing:

Blend butter and flour. Place on the range and stir until butter is melted. Add milk, stirring all the time till mixture is thick. Add salt and pepper. Separate the whites of the eggs from the yolks. Chop the whites fine, and add to the dressing. Arrange slices of toast on a hot platter, pour the dressing over them; force the yolks through a ricer onto the toast and dressing; serve hot.

OMELETTE.

Omelettes are of two classes: The French and the puffy. There are many variations, but all belong to one of the two classes.

The number of yolks should exceed the number of whites in an omelette. If this rule is observed they will be more tender and of a looser texture.

PLAIN OMELETTE.

Materials:

3 eggs.	2 tablesponfuls clear bacon fat or 1 tablespoonful butter.
½ teaspoonful salt.	
Dash of pepper.	
	3 tablespoonfuls hot water.

Way of Preparing:

Beat eggs very light, add salt, pepper and hot water. Heat the omelette pan, and add bacon fat or butter. Cook slowly. When thickened and browned underneath, put in grate of oven to finish the top. When the top will not adhere to the finger, the omelette is done. Fold and serve on hot platter.

Quantity:

Will serve four people.

FRENCH OMELETTE.

Materials:

4 eggs.	Pinch pepper.
5 tablespoonfuls ice water.	1 teaspoonful sugar.
½ teaspoonful salt.	1 heaping tablespoonful butter.
2 egg yolks.	

Way of Preparing:

Place the eggs in a bowl and beat with a fork until they are thoroughly mixed and then strain them, add the water, salt, pepper and sugar. Melt the butter in a frying pan, pour in the egg mixture. Set over the fire for a minute, then with a spatula, separate the cooked portion from the frying pan and gently move it back and forth so that the uncooked portions may come in contact with the pan. When it becomes creamy and begins to set, begin at the side of the pan, next to the handle, with a spatula, and fold the omelette over. Turn onto a hot platter and serve immediately.

Quantity:
This will serve four people.

HYGIENIC EGGS.

Materials:

6 eggs. *½ cup white sauce.
6 round slices of toast. Salt and pepper.
1 cup finely-chopped
  chicken.

Way of Preparing:
Heat the chicken in the sauce and spread each slice of toast with the mixture. Beat the whites of the eggs until very stiff, pile the beaten whites on the rounds of toast in the shape of nests. Carefully place one unbroken yolk in each nest. Cook in a moderate oven until set. Dust with salt and pepper and serve at once.

Quantity:
This will serve six.

*Recipe for white sauce will be found under "White Sauce Omelette."

PUFF OMELETTE.

Materials:

4 eggs. 6 tablespoonfuls water.
2 yolks. ½ teaspoonful salt.
Pinch pepper. 1 tablespoonful butter.

Way of Preparing:
Beat the whites of the eggs until dry and the yolks until they are thick and of a lemon color. Add the water, salt and pepper to the yolks. Mix thoroughly and then fold the whites into the yolk mixture. Put the butter in a frying pan and when it is hot put in the mixture. Let it stand in a moderate heat for two minutes, place in a hot oven and cook until set. Remove from the oven, cut across the center at right angles to the handle, turn on a hot platter and serve.

Quantity:
This will serve four persons.

Note.—Either French or puff omelette may be varied by the use of fillings, or garnishings, or both.

A Header in "the Land of Pillsbury's Best"

WHITE SAUCE OMELETTE.

Materials:

½ cup milk.
½ cup cream.
1 tablespoonful butter.
5 eggs.
2 tablespoonfuls flour.
½ teaspoonful salt.
1 teaspoonful sugar.
Pinch pepper.
2 tablespoonfuls butter.

Way of Preparing:

Make a white sauce of the milk, cream, flour, salt and one tablespoonful of butter, beat the egg yolks and stir them into the sauce, then add the stiffly-beaten whites of the eggs, folding them in carefully.

Then add sugar and pepper. Melt the two tablespoonfuls of butter in the omelette pan and cook as a puff omelette.

Finely chopped ham, tongue, chicken, sweetbreads or any cold meat may be added to this omelette. If used, add them to the white sauce with the yolks of the eggs.

Quantity:

This will serve five persons.

SCRAMBLED EGGS.

Materials:

6 eggs.
2 tablespoonfuls milk.
2 tablespoonfuls water.
½ teaspoonful salt.
¼ teaspoonful white pepper.
2 tablespoonfuls butter.

Way of Preparing:

Beat the eggs without separating, add the other ingredients, mixing thoroughly. Strain the mixture. Melt the butter in a frying pan and pour in the mixture. Stir constantly until it is soft and creamy throughout.

Serve at once.

This dish may be varied by the addition of any finely chopped cooked meat. If so, it should be mixed with the eggs just before taking from the fire.

Quantity:

This will serve four persons.

·FISH & OYSTERS

"From the rude sea's enraged and foaming mouth."
—Twelfth Night.

First.—Catch your fish.

Second.—Serve your soup course.

The fish course which follows the soup need not be very substantial as it is not intended to satisfy the hunger. But it must always be associated with some kind of fish, even if you have to buy the fish.

It may consist of any large fish boiled or baked, fish-cutlets, small fish fried or planked fish.

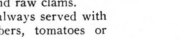

Shell-fish may also be served at this point of the dinner, as lobsters boiled, soft shell crabs, boiled or fried, oysters raw and raw clams.

Potatoes in some form are always served with fish, and either raw cucumbers, tomatoes or radishes are passed.

If the fish is served with sauce, potatoes should be offered, fried in some form such as croquettes, cakes or straws.

In serving fish at dinner the light-meated ones are preferred, because they are more easily digested than those with dark meat.

BAKED FISH.

Materials:

4 lbs. fish.
1 tablespoonful salt.
1 pint bread crumbs.
4 tablespoonfuls melted butter.
1 lemon.
1 tablespoonful minced parsley.

2 tablespoonfuls grated onion.
¼ teaspoonful pepper.
½ teaspoonful salt.
1 cup raw oysters.
Slices of fat pork.

Way of Preparing:

Have a four-pound fish, with the head on; wash it thoroughly, and sprinkle with one tablespoonful of salt. Put in the ice box and leave it there two hours.

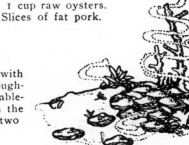

Make a stuffing of one cup of crumbs, the parsley, grated onion, melted butter, lemon juice, grated rind of lemon, salt, pepper and raw oysters chopped.

Fill the body of the fish with this stuffing, sew up the opening and skewer into any desired shape. Place on a baking sheet, cover with slices of fat pork and bake in a hot oven.

When the fish begins to brown baste it with hot water and reduce the heat of the oven.

Bake slowly, basting every ten minutes. At the end of forty minutes remove the pork, cover the fish with a white sauce, sprinkle with bread crumbs and bake until the crumbs are brown. When done remove to a hot platter and garnish with fried oysters, parsley, or slices of lemon and parsley.

Quantity:

This will serve six people.

BROILED LOBSTER.

Materials:

1 live lobster.   Sliced lemon.

½ cup melted butter.

Way of Preparing:

Begin at the mouth of the lobster and with a sharp knife split the lobster through the body and tail.

Open and remove the liver, stomach and intestinal vein. Brush the lobster well with melted butter. Put on the broiler, flesh-side up, and broil ten minutes.

Turn shell-side and broil eight minutes. Serve with melted butter and sliced lemon.

Quantity:

This will serve two persons.

CODFISH BALLS.

Materials:

1 cup cooked codfish.   Flour.

2 eggs.   Fried potatoes.

1 cup cracker crumbs.   Parsley.

Fat.

1 cup mashed potatoes prepared as for the table.

Way of Preparing:

Mash the codfish very smooth. Add the potatoes and one egg well beaten, and mix thoroughly. Form into small balls about the size of an English walnut. Roll in flour, then in egg, then in cracker crumbs, and fry in deep fat.

Drain, pile on a platter in a nice pyramid; garnish with fried potatoes and parsley and serve.

Quantity:

This will serve five persons

CREAMED FISH.

Materials:

2 cups cold fish.
1 cup hot milk.
1 bay leaf.
½ teaspoonful onion
   juice.
2 tablespoonfuls butter.

2 tablespoonfuls flour.
½ teaspoonful salt.
¼ teaspoonful white
   pepper.
½ cup fine crumbs.

Way of Preparing:

Make a sauce by creaming the flour and butter and adding them to the hot milk. Put this in a double boiler and add the salt, pepper, onion juice and bay leaf. Stir until as thick as cream. Now cover the bottom of a baking dish with some of the cold fish, flaked, and pour over it half the sauce. Then put in another layer of fish and on that pour the remainder of the sauce.

Sprinkle all with crumbs, dot with butter and brown in a moderately hot oven.

Any kind of cold fish may be used.

Quantity:

This will serve six persons.

CURRIED LOBSTER.

Materials:

2 two-pound lobsters.
2 teaspoonfuls lemon
   juice.
½ teaspoonful curry
   powder.
2 tablespoonfuls butter.

1 tablespoonful flour.
1 cup scalded milk.
1 cup cracker crumbs.
½ teaspoonful salt.
¼ teaspoonful pepper.

Way of Preparing:

Cream the butter and flour and add the scalded milk, then add the lemon juice, curry powder, salt and pepper. Remove the lobster meat from the shells and cut into half-inch cubes. Add the latter to the sauce. Refill the lobster shells, cover with buttered crumbs, and bake until the crumbs are brown. Instead of the shells you may use a buttered baking dish.

Quantity:

This will serve six persons.

FISH CHOWDER.

Materials:

2½ lbs. fresh fish, sliced.
4 large potatoes, sliced.
1 cup milk.

½ lb. salt pork.
1 large onion.
3 sea biscuits.

Way of Preparing:

Cut the pork in cubes and put them in a frying pan over the fire. When they are frying put in the onion sliced, and fry it brown. Butter a small kettle and put in a layer of the sliced potatoes, then one of fish, then a layer of pork and onions. Sprinkle with salt and pepper. Put in another layer of potatoes, one of fish, one of pork and onions, sprinkle again with salt and pepper, and put in one more layer of potatoes. Pour over all the milk and enough water to nearly cover it. Now place the cover on the kettle and let it boil slowly for twenty-five minutes. Remove the cover and place on top of the chowder two or three sea-biscuits, broken in pieces. Replace the cover and let the chowder barely simmer ten minutes longer. Then serve immediately.

Quantity:

This will serve eight persons.

Note.—Oyster and clam chowder are prepared in the same manner.

FISH CROQUETTES.

Materials:

2 cups cold fish.	2 tablespoonfuls flour.
1 cup milk.	2 tablespoonfuls butter.
1 teaspoonful salt.	½ teaspoonful pepper.
1 cup crumbs.	2 eggs.
Parsley.	Lemons.
Fat.	

Way of Preparing:

Cream the flour and butter. Put the milk in a double boiler, and when it is at the boiling point add the flour and butter. Stir until it is smooth and thick, and add the salt, pepper and fish, flaked. Spread on a platter and let it cool. Then shape, roll in flour, egg and crumbs and fry in deep fat. Arrange on a hot dish, and garnish with parsley and sliced lemon.

Quantity:

This will serve six persons.

FISH PREMIER, WITH PREMIER SAUCE.

Materials:

4 lbs. fish.	2 doz. large oysters.
½ cup melted butter.	Sliced lemon.
Salt and pepper.	Watercress.
1 cup crumbs.	

Way of Preparing:

Remove the head and tail of the fish. Skin and bone it, leaving two oblong pieces. Lay one of

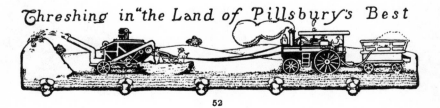

Threshing in "the Land of Pillsbury's Best

the pieces on a greased baking sheet in the baking pan, cover with half of the oysters. Sprinkle thickly with crumbs and pour over them one-half of your melted butter. Then cover it with the other half of the fish. Place the remaining oysters on top of the fish, sprinkle with salt and pepper. Place the remaining crumbs on the oysters and pour the rest of the butter over the crumbs. Put into a moderate oven and brown. When done slip it carefully onto a hot platter, garnish with watercress and sliced lemon, and serve with a

Premier Sauce,

made of—

¼ cup of butter.	¼ teaspoonful salt.
Yolk of one egg.	1-3 cup boiling water.
Juice of ½ lemon.	A pinch of white pepper.

Cook in a double boiler for six minutes and serve in a sauceboat.

Quantity:

This will easily serve six persons.

LOBSTER, NEWBURG STYLE.

Materials:

2 large lobsters, boiled.	1 wineglass sherry wine.
½ teaspoonful salt.	½ pint cream.
¼ teaspoonful white pepper.	3 egg yolks.
2 large truffles, sliced.	2 tablespoonfuls butter.
	Toast.

Way of Preparing:

Cut the lobster meat in inch pieces, put them in a saucepan with the butter, and place over a hot fire. Add the salt, pepper and truffles, and cook five minutes. Then add the sherry and cook three minutes longer.

Beat the yolks of the eggs and whip them into the cream, now add this slowly to the lobster and cook three minutes. Serve on toast.

Quantity:

This will serve eight persons.

OYSTERS AND MACARONI.

Materials:

1 pint oysters.	2 tablespoonfuls flour.
½ lb. macaroni.	1 tablespoonful butter.
1 teaspoonful salt.	1 cup milk.
½ teaspoonful pepper.	½ cup crumbs.

Way of Preparing:

Make a sauce of the butter, flour, milk, salt and pepper. Break the macaroni in inch pieces and boil them twenty-five minutes in water. Then wash them in cold water and drain. Put a layer of the boiled and washed macaroni in a buttered pudding dish, cover it with oysters and the latter with sauce, repeat and cover all with crumbs. Dot with butter and bake twenty-five minutes in a hot oven. Serve from the baking dish.

Quantity:

This dish will serve six persons.

PIGS IN BLANKETS.

Materials:

Large oysters.
Thin slices of breakfast bacon.
Lemon.
Melted butter.

Pepper.
Toothpicks.
Celery.
Toast.

Way of Preparing:

Wash and dry the oysters. Have as many strips of bacon as you have oysters. Place a strip of bacon lengthwise on your left hand, lay an oyster across the upper end. Now begin to roll toward the tips of your fingers. When the oyster is inclosed in the bacon, skewer the latter with a small toothpick. When you have prepared all the oysters in this manner, sprinkle with pepper, dip in the melted butter and broil. Serve on hot toast with celery, and garnish the platter with lemon and the white leaves of the celery.

Quantity:

Allow four to each person.

PLANKED FISH.

Materials:

4 lbs. white fish.
1 lemon.
1 teaspoonful salt.

½ cup butter.
½ teaspoonful pepper.
1 cup boiling water.

Way of Preparing:

Remove the head from the fish and have it split from head to tail, so that it can be flattened out on the plank. Take care not to split the skin. Have the plank very hot and brush with butter. Place the fish, skin-side down on the board and tack it firmly in place.

Put it in a moderately hot oven and at the end of five minutes take a small brush and give the fish a bath, using the other ingredients, which you have made into a sauce for basting. Continue this every ten minutes for thirty-five minutes. Then remove from the oven, place the plank on a platter and serve at once. Garnish the platter so as to cover the plank, but never remove the fish from it when serving.

The plank should be of hardwood (oak) sixteen inches long, twelve inches wide and one and a half inches thick.

Quantity:

This dish will serve six persons.

G A M E

Let's carve him as a dish fit for the gods,
Not hew him as a Carcass.

—Julius Caesar.

Since the days of Nimrod, the first hunter,
every household has been stirred to its founda-
tion every now and then by a male member stalk-
ing in with some wild thing "plucked from the
forest" and demanding that "you cook it."

Then it is that the faithful wife trembles with
emotion. All eyes are upon her. Her ability
in the estimation of her husband will rise or fall
with that goose.

BROILED QUAIL.

Materials:

Quail.	Salt.
Melted butter.	Pepper.
Lemon.	Parsley.
Currant jelly.	Toast.

Way of Preparing:

Singe and wipe clean; beginning at the neck on
the back, split and lay open. Remove the inside
contents, then remove the breastbone and wipe
clean inside. Sprinkle with salt and pepper, brush
with melted butter, and broil for fifteen minutes
on a brisk fire. Turn frequently. When done serve,
garnished with parsley on toast or with currant
jelly.

BROILED VENISON STEAK.

Materials:

Venison steak.	Pepper.
Butter.	Salt.

Way of Preparing:

Wipe the steak with a cloth wrung out of cold
water. Place the steak in a hot buttered broiler
and broil with a clear brisk fire. Turn every ten
seconds for the first minute. After that turn occasionally until cooked on both sides.

Venison should always be served rare. Roast
venison is prepared the same as roast lamb.

ROAST WILD DUCK.

Materials:

I wild duck.   Salt and pepper.
4 strips salt pork.   Currant jelly.
½ cup water.

Way of Preparing:

Clean and truss the duck and sprinkle with salt
and pepper. Cover the breast with the slices of
salt pork. Place on the rack in the dripping pan
and pour the water in the pan. Put in a hot oven
and cook half an hour, basting every five minutes
with the drippings from the pan. Remove the bacon and serve with currant jelly.

Domestic Duck

is cooked in the same manner, but requires one
hour and a quarter of cooking.

Stuffing

is used the same as for chicken or turkey or you
may stuff with apples, peeled and cut in eighths.
If no stuffing is used, a whole onion placed in the
body of the duck, while cooking, will improve the
flavor and should be removed before serving.

ICE CREAM
And
ICES

Then farewell heat and welcome frost.
Merchant of Venice.

Ice creams are divided into two different classes; the Neapolitan and the Philadelphian. The former contains a large proportion of eggs, has a pronounced custard flavor and its color is lemon-yellow. The Philadelphian has a creamy shade and the flavor of sweet cream.

The first operation in making either kind is the cooking, either with or without the eggs. In case of the Neapolitan, strain the yolks of the eggs and beat until thick and lemon-colored, then add the sugar and beat again. Then add the stiffly-beaten whites and beat again. Add the milk and cream and cook in a double boiler until it coats a spoon without running. Stir constantly and be careful not to let it curdle. Strain again through a wine sieve and let it cool. Flavoring is added either before or after cooking. This depends upon the kind of flavor used, but the process thus far is the same with all Neapolitan creams.

The Philadelphian cream is sometimes made of fresh, uncooked cream, if a very light, fluffy cream is wanted. Cook the cream in a double boiler, with cold water in the outer pan. Bring to a boil, and then remove from the fire. Add the flavoring and the sugar and stir until the latter is melted. Strain and cool. Now it is ready for the freezer.

In adding fruit to the creams, (such as peaches, pineapple, plums, oranges or apricots) it must be cut into small dice, sprinkled with sugar and allowed to stand two hours.

Berries must be mashed, sugared and mixed with the frozen cream. Always thoroughly chill the cream before freezing it. It is then smoother and the chilling makes it freeze more rapidly and easily.

FREEZING.

Pour the chilled cream into the freezer. Place the freezer in the pail and pack with ice nearly to the top. Sprinkle coarse salt uniformly on the ice as you pack it into the bucket. Cover and fasten the can and turn it slowly until it becomes difficult to turn. Open the can and remove the dasher. Scrape the cream from the sides of the can. Mix until smooth, close the can and drain off the brine. Add fresh ice and salt, covering the entire can. Wrap a blanket around the freezer and let it stand two hours.

In very hot weather renew the salt and ice three times and keep the blanket cold and wet with the brine from the freezer.

ANGEL FOOD ICE CREAM.

Materials:

Whites of 4 eggs.
½ cup sugar.
1 quart whipped cream.

1 teaspoonful almond extract.

Way of Preparing:

Beat the eggs very stiff and stir in the sugar. fold in the whipped cream and the flavoring extract. Line a mold with New York Ice Cream and fill the center with this mixture.

Pack in salt and ice and let it stand three hours.

Quantity:

This will serve six persons.

*The recipe for New York Ice Cream you will find elsewhere herein.

BURNT ALMOND ICE CREAM.

Materials:

1 quart cream.
6 eggs.

1 lb. sugar.
4 oz. shelled almonds.
1 tablespoonful vanilla.

Way of Preparing:

Blanch the almonds and brown them in the oven. Pound to a paste in a mortar, adding a little sugar and cream to make a paste.

Mix the eggs, sugar and cream, and add the almond paste. Then freeze according to directions under "Freezing." Adding a tablespoonful of Caramel will produce a richer color.

Quantity:

This will serve six persons.

CARAMEL ICE CREAM.

Materials:

1 quart cream.
6 eggs.
1 lb. sugar.

1 tablespoonful vanilla extract.
4 tablespoonfuls caramel.

Way of Preparing:

Prepare the custard as directed. Freeze as per directions for "Freezing" and add the caramel and vanilla when beating down the half frozen cream.

Quantity:

This will serve six persons.

CHESTNUT ICE CREAM.

Materials:

1 pint cream.　　　　　1 lb. sugar.
1 pint milk.　　　　　 4 oz. chestnut meats.
6 eggs.　　　　　　　 2 tablespoonfuls vanilla
　　　　　　　　　　　　 extract.

Way of Preparing:

Use the Italian chestnuts. Boil them until soft. Peel and reduce them to a pulp in a mortar, adding a little sugar and cream enough to form a paste.

Prepare the sugar, eggs and cream and add the chestnut paste. Then cook and freeze as directed under "Freezing."

Quantity:

This will serve eight persons.

CHOCOLATE ICE CREAM.

Materials:

1 pint cream.　　　　　5 ozs. chocolate,
1 pint milk.　　　　　 ¾ lb. sugar.
6 eggs.　　　　　　　 1 teaspoonful cinnamon
　　　　　　　　　　　　 extract.

Way of Preparing:

Melt the chocolate and add the cinnamon extract. Make and cook the custard as directed in general remarks on Ice Creams; then add to it the chocolate while both are hot. Cool, chill and freeze as directed in "Freezing." To make

Caramel Chocolate Ice Cream

omit the cinnamon extract and use instead three tablespoonfuls of the prepared caramel syrup, recipe for which you will find elsewhere in this volume.

Quantity:

This will serve six persons.

COFFEE ICE CREAM.

Materials:

1 quart cream.　　　　1 cup ground coffee.
1 quart milk.　　　　 1 teaspoonful vanilla
9 eggs.　　　　　　　 extract whipped
1½ lbs. sugar.　　　　 cream.

Way of Preparing:

Pour the milk over the coffee and bring to a boil. Boil slowly ten minutes and then allow it to settle and cool. Drain off the milk and strain it, add enough more milk to make one quart. Add this to the cream, eggs and sugar, make a custard as explained elsewhere herein, and freeze according to directions in "Freezing." Serve with whipped cream.

Quantity:

This will serve ten persons.

MAPLE PERFECT.

Materials:

4 eggs.　　　　　　　 1 teaspoonful almond
½ pint hot maple syrup.　 extract.
1 pint thick cream.　　 Salt and ice.

Way of Preparing:

Beat the eggs slightly and pour on them slowly the maple syrup. Cook until the mixture thickens and cool it, then add the extract, remove from the range, cool, and then add the cream, beaten until stiff. Mold, pack in salt and ice and let stand four hours.

Quantity:

This will serve six persons.

NESSELRODE PUDDING.

Materials:

3 cups cream.	2 cups milk.
2 cups sugar.	½ cup pineapple syrup.
5 egg yolks.	1 pint prepared Italian
1 pinch salt.	chestnuts.
½ cup Sultana raisins.	1 cup candied fruits.

Way of Preparing:

Make a custard of the milk, sugar, eggs and salt, according to directions elsewhere herein, strain and cool. Add the pineapple syrup, cream and chestnuts. Then freeze, as directed elsewhere herein. Line a two-quart mold with part of the mixture and to the remainder add one cup candied fruits, minced, one-half cup sultana raisins and six chestnuts, chopped. Fill the mold. Pack in ice, and let it stand three hours. To "prepare" the chestnuts, shell and boil until very soft, then pass them through a potato ricer.

Quantity:

This will serve twelve persons.

NEW YORK ICE CREAM.

Materials:

2 cups milk.	1 tablespoonful gelatine.
3 cups cream.	
1 cup sugar.	1 tablespoonful vanilla extract.
1 pinch salt.	
Yolks of 7 eggs.	1 tablespoonful lemon extract.
	Warm water.

Way of Preparing:

Make a custard of the milk, sugar, eggs and salt. Bring it to a boil. Remove from the fire and add the gelatine, melted in a little warm water, cool, strain and flavor. Whip the cream, add it to the custard and freeze according to directions elsewhere herein.

Quantity:

This will serve eight persons.

NOUGAT ICE CREAM.

Materials:

2 cups milk.	¼ cup pistachios.
1 cup sugar.	5 egg whites.
5 egg yolks.	¼ cup filberts.
½ teaspoonful salt.	¼ cup English walnuts.
2 cups thick cream.	¼ cup almond meats.
1 tablespoonful vanilla	¼ cup hickory nuts.
extract.	1 teaspoonful almond extract.

Way of Preparing:

Make a custard of the milk, sugar, egg yolks and salt, as per directions elsewhere herein, and strain and cool. Beat the cream and add it. Then add the nut-meats chopped fine, the whites of the eggs, well-beaten and the flavoring extracts. Freeze according to directions elsewhere herein, and allow it to stand four hours.

Quantity:
This will serve ten persons.

ORANGE ICE.

Materials:

1 quart water.	Grated rind of one
1 pint sugar.	orange.
1 pint orange juice.	Grated rind of one
¼ pint lemon juice.	lemon.

Way of Preparing:
Make a syrup of the sugar and water. Boil fifteen minutes and add the orange juice, lemon juice, orange peel and lemon rind.

Freeze (according to directions elsewhere herein) and serve in glasses.

Quantity:
This will serve twelve persons.

PINEAPPLE MOUSSE.

Materials:

1 tablespoonful granulated gelatine.	2 tablespoonfuls lemon juice.
¼ cup cold water.	1½ cups sugar.
1 cup pineapple syrup.	1 quart whipped cream.

Way of Preparing:
Soak the gelatine in the cold water. Heat the pineapple syrup and add the lemon juice, sugar and gelatine; strain and cool. When the mixture thickens fold in the whipped cream. Mold, pack in salt and ice and let stand four hours.

Quantity:
This will serve six persons.

PISTACHIO ICE CREAM.

Materials:

1 quart cream.	1 oz. bitter almonds.
6 eggs.	1 teaspoonful vanilla
1 lb. sugar.	extract.
4 oz. pistachio nuts.	Rosewater.

Way of Preparing:
Pound the nuts in a mortar and add a few drops of rosewater. Gradually add one cup of cream and one of sugar. Mix all the ingredients, cook as per general directions herein and freeze as directed under "Freezing."

Quantity:
This will serve six persons.

Elevators in "the Land of Pillsbury's Best."

PINEAPPLE ICE.

Materials:

4 cups water.   4 cups ice-water.
2 cups sugar.   1 can grated pineapple.
Juice of 6 lemons.

Way of Preparing:

Make a syrup of the water and sugar and boil for fifteen minutes. Add the pineapple and lemon juice. Cool and add the icewater. Freeze **until** mushy, using half ice and half salt.

Quantity:

This will serve twelve persons.

QUEEN'S ICE CREAM.

Materials:

1 quart cream.   2 egg whites.
¾ lb. sugar.   1 oz. sponge cake.
6 egg yolks.   1 tablespoonful **vanilla**
                                   extract.

Way of Preparing:

Beat the yolks to a cream and add all the sugar but two tablespoonfuls. Beat it very hard and thoroughly. Beat the two whites of eggs until stiff enough to cut. Add the two tablespoonfuls of sugar and beat again. Roll and sift the sponge cake, which must be quite stale. Put the cream, sugar, vanilla and egg yolks in a double boiler and cook as directed in general remarks about "Ice Creams." Then strain and add the cake dust and vanilla. Freeze according to directions elsewhere. When you remove the dasher from the freezer add the beaten whites of the eggs. Work until smooth. Cover and pack as directed elsewhere.

Macaroon crumbs may be substituted for **the** sponge cake.

Quantity:

This will serve six persons.

ROMAN PUNCH.

Materials:

*2 quarts pineapple ice.   4 whites of eggs.
½ pint Jamaica rum.   2 tablespoonfuls vanilla.
½ lb. sugar.   1 pint champagne.

Way of Preparing:

Put the sugar in a saucepan and add one cup of water. Boil until it will form a ball when dipped in water and rolled between the thumb and finger. Beat the whites of the eggs very stiff, and gradually add to them this hot syrup, stirring all the time. Stir until cold. Mix the rum and Vanilla with the pineapple ice and then beat in the egg mixture, whip in the champagne and serve immediately.

Quantity:

This will serve twenty-four persons.

*The recipe for pineapple ice you will find elsewhere in this book.

STRAWBERRY ICE CREAM.

Materials:

1 quart berries.	½ cup cream.
1½ cups sugar.	1 pint scalded cream.

Way of Preparing:

Mash berries and sprinkle with one cup of sugar. Let stand ½ hour. Strain through coarse cheese cloth, pressing until only the seeds remain. Dissolve ½ cup sugar in the scalded cream and when cooled add to strawberry juice. Turn into freezer. When frozen to mush, add ½ cup plain cream, recover and freeze hard.

Quantity:

This serves six.

TOM AND JERRY.

Materials:

1½ cup milk.	3 cups cream.
1 cup sugar.	3 tablespoonfuls brandy.
6 egg yolks.	
1 teaspoonful vanilla extract.	2 tablespoonfuls rum.
	1 pinch salt.

Way of Preparing:

Make a custard of the milk, sugar, eggs, salt and vanilla, as mentioned in general remarks on Ice Cream herein. Half freeze, add the rum and brandy and finish freezing.

Quantity:

This will serve eight persons.

VANILLA ICE CREAM.

Materials:

1 pint cream.	1 tablespoonful vanilla extract.
1 pint milk.	
1 lb. sugar.	9 eggs.

Way of Preparing:

Prepare and cook the ingredients as given in the general directions about Ice-Cream and freeze as directed in "Freezing" also herein.

Quantity:

This will serve six persons.

INVALID DISHES

Such dainties to them, their health it might hurt:
It's like sending them ruffles when wanting a shirt.
—Goldsmith.

The greatest weight is to be attached to the preparation of food for the sick. Oftentimes the diet is of more importance than the drug. Entire wholesomeness of food, the best preparation possible, and prompt and dainty service are necessary requisites.

Do not consult the patient as to the menu, for the various surprises will help to tickle his appetite.

First prepare the tray with a spotless cloth or napkin folded just to cover; then select the smallest, prettiest dishes from the cupboard, being careful to place everything in an orderly and convenient manner. Serve hot foods on hot dishes, cold foods on cold dishes.

For feverish patients, cold water mixed with fruit juices is refreshing and beneficial.

Pillsbury's Vitos gruel is most excellent for those needing a food readily assimilated and still full of nourishment. It is non-heat-producing, and therefore valuable for inflammatory and feverish conditions.

ALMOND SOUP.

Materials:

½ lb. almonds.

1 pint milk.

2 tablespoonfuls sugar.

½ teaspoonful salt.

1 pint hot milk.

Way of Preparing:

Blanch the almonds and pound them in a mortar, gradually adding one pint of milk. When you have pounded it to a smooth paste, and used up all the milk, strain it by squeezing it through a piece of cheesecloth. To the scalded milk add sugar and salt. Now add it to the almond mixture and bring it to the boiling point. Serve hot.

BROILED BEEF JUICE.

Materials:

2 lbs. lean steak from the top of the round.

Salt, pepper.

Way of Preparing:

Remove any visible fat from the steak, broil over a brisk fire for four minutes, turning it frequently. Cut in pieces about one inch square and gash each piece two or three times. Place in a meat press and squeeze the juice into a hot cup. Season to taste and serve hot.

CHICKEN BROTH.

Materials:

1 4-lb. fowl.

2 quarts water.

Seasoning.

Way of Preparing:

Joint the fowl and skin it, removing all visible fat. Break the bones, place in a saucepan, and pour the water over it. Let stand one hour. Bring it slowly to the boiling point and simmer for three hours. Strain, cool, remove all fat and season to taste. This is served either hot or cold.

BARLEY WATER.

Materials:

2 tablespoonfuls pearl barley.

1 quart water.

Way of Preparing:

Put the barley over the fire in cold water, let it come to a boil and cook five minutes, then drain off the water and rinse the barley in cold water. Then return it to the fire and add one quart of water. Bring it to a boil and simmer until reduced one-half. It may be sweetened and flavored if desired.

OATMEAL GRUEL.

Materials:

½ cup oatmeal. Sugar.
3 pints boiling water. Cream.
1 teaspoonful salt.

Way of Preparing:

Add the salt to the boiling water, stir in the oatmeal and cook for two and one-half hours in a double boiler. Remove from the fire and strain. When preparing it for a patient, use half a cup of gruel mixed with half a cup of thin cream, two tablespoonfuls of boiling water and sugar to taste.

A pinch of nutmeg or cinnamon is also sometimes added. Other gruels are prepared in the same manner.

CHICKEN CUSTARD.

Materials:

½ cup bread crumbs. 2 tablespoonfuls chopped breast of chicken.
2 egg yolks.
Pinch of celery salt.
  Pinch of salt.
  1 cup milk.

Way of Preparing:

Take the crumbs from the center of a stale loaf and add to them the finely chopped chicken. Beat the yolks until well mixed, and add to them the salt, celery salt and milk. Pour this over the other ingredients mixing thoroughly. Fill a custard cup with the mixture, place it in a pan of hot water and bake in a moderate oven until set. Serve hot.

FLAXSEED LEMONADE.

Materials:

2 tablespoonfuls flaxseed. 1 cup sugar.
  Grated rind and juice of three lemons.
1 quart boiling water.

Way of Preparing:

Blanch the flaxseed, and add the boiling water, let it simmer for three quarters of an hour, then add the sugar and lemon rind. Let it stand fifteen minutes. Strain and add the lemon juice. Serve either hot or cold. For a bad cough, take a tablespoonful every hour.

RICE WATER.

Materials:

2 tablespoonfuls rice. 1 teaspoonful salt.
1 quart boiling water. Flavoring, sugar.

Way of Preparing:

Blanch the rice, drain and add the boiling water. Cook for an hour and a quarter, keeping it simmering only. Then strain, add the salt and use when needed. Sweetening and flavoring to taste may be added if desired. Rice water is also used to dilute milk and is sometimes combined with chicken broth.

SYLLABUB.

Materials:

4 egg yolks.	1 pint milk.
1 tablespoonful flour.	¾ cup sugar.
1 teaspoonful flavoring extract.	1 pint whipped cream.

Way of Preparing:

Mix half the sugar with the flour, bring the milk to a boiling point and add sugar and flour to it. Cook in a double boiler ten minutes. Beat the egg yolks and add the other half of the sugar to them. Now add this to the milk mixture, cook five minutes, stirring all the time. Remove from the fire and add the flavoring extract. Let the mixture get cold. When serving fill a tumbler half full of this custard and finish filling with whipped cream.

Note:

Other dishes equally acceptable to invalids are—
Egg Nogg,
Sherry and Egg.
Tenderloin Steak with Beef Juice.
Broiled Squabs.
Junket.
Raw Beef Sandwich.
Broiled Spring Chicken,
Hot Orange or Pineapple Juice served in a cup, etc., etc.

WINE WHEY.

Materials:

1 pint milk.	½ pint sherry wine.

Way of Preparing:

Heat the milk to a boiling point, then add the sherry. Bring it again to the boiling point and strain through cheesecloth.

MEATS

"They that have no other meat,
Bread and butter are glad to eat."
"A good fire makes a good cook."

Next to bread, meat forms the principal food on our tables. We not only eat more meat as a nation, but provide other nations with more than anyone else. Beef, veal, mutton and pork are the meats of our households. The vast majority of our housekeepers are not sufficiently well informed as to the proper way of cutting up an animal. Hence they rely entirely too much upon their butchers in the purchase of their meats. It must be assumed that the readers of these recipes are measurably familiar with that part of the knowledge required to be a good buyer of meat at retail. If not, there are more extensive works on cooking for acquiring it.

The cheaper parts of a first-class animal may be prepared to furnish far better dishes than the high-priced portions of an inferior animal; in other words, a stew from the forequarter of a first-class animal will be better than a roast from the loin of an inferior animal, and it will be cheaper.

BAKED LIVER LARDED.
Materials:

1 calf's liver.	2 cups boiling water.
½ lb. fat salt pork.	2 tablespoonfuls butter.
1 carrot.	2 tablespoonfuls flour.
1 onion.	½ teaspoonful salt.
1 red pepper.	Juice of 1 lemon.
½ bayleaf.	

Way of Preparing:
Skewer the liver into shape and lard it with strips of the fat pork. Surround it with the vegetables chopped fine. Add to the boiling water the seasonings, and pour this over the liver. Cover and bake for one hour and a half. Uncover and bake fifteen minutes longer. Remove from the pan, add the lemon juice to the liquor, strain over the liver and serve.

Quantity:
This will serve four persons.

BEEFSTEAK PIE.

Materials:

2 lbs. round steak ½
inch thick.

1 onion sliced.

1 heaping tablespoonful
flour.

2 tablespoonfuls butter.

2 medium potatoes
sliced thin.

1 teaspoonful salt.

½ teaspoonful pepper.

Way of Preparing:

Cut the steak into strips one and one-half inch long and one inch wide, place the strips in a sauce pan, cover with boiling water, add the sliced onion, and simmer until the meat is tender. Remove the meat, discard the onion, add the potatoes to the liquor and parboil six minutes. Then remove the potatoes. Now measure the liquor and add enough boiling water to make one pint and add the seasonings. Cream the butter and flour together, add it to the liquor and cook five minutes. In the bottom of a pudding dish, place a layer of one-half the parboiled potatoes and on top of this layer arrange the meat, placing the other half of the potatoes in a layer on top of it. Pour over this sufficient gravy to entirely cover the contents of the baking dish. Now let it cool, when cool cover it with a crust and bake in a hot oven.

The crust is made as follows:

Materials:

1 cup flour.

1 rounding tablespoonful butter.

1 rounding tablespoonful lard.

½ teaspoonful salt.

1 teaspoonful baking powder.

Milk.

Way of Preparing:

Sift the flour, baking powder and salt, cream the butter and lard together and combine them with the dry ingredients, mixing them thoroughly with your finger tips. Now add enough milk to make a soft dough, roll it out about one-quarter of an inch thick, and cover with it the contents of your pudding dish.

Quantity:

This will serve six persons.

BEEF LOAF.

Materials:

3 lbs. lean beef.

½ lb. raw ham.

3 eggs, well beaten.

3 soda crackers rolled fine.

1 teaspoonful salt.

1 teaspoonful pepper.

3 tablespoonfuls cream.

6 hard boiled eggs.

Way of Preparing:

Chop the beef and ham very fine and then add the salt and pepper, the cracker crumbs, the well beaten eggs, and the cream. Mix all these together perfectly, grease a bread pan, thoroughly, and press half the mixture into it firmly. Trim each end of your hard boiled eggs so as to make a flat surface, then put them on top of the mixture in the bread-pan, placing them in a row end to end. Now pack on top the balance of your meat, pressing it down firmly. Cover and bake in a moderate oven one hour. Uncover and bake half an hour longer. Serve either hot or cold in slices.

Quantity:

This will serve ten persons.

BEEF TONGUE PIQUANT.

Materials:

1 fresh tongue.	1 onion.
1 carrot.	1 stalk celery.
1 red pepper.	1 teaspoonful salt.

Way of Preparing:

Place the tongue in a kettle and cover with boiling water, adding the vegetables and seasoning. Cover and cook until tender. Take the tongue from the kettle and remove the skin and root. Put back into the kettle and reheat. Serve it sliced into half inch slices accompanied by a

SAUCE

made of the following:

Materials:

4 tablespoonfuls of flour.	2 tablespoonfuls butter.
¾ cup brown stock.	1 teaspoonful salt.
½ teaspoonful paprika.	2 tablespoonfuls lemon-juice.
1 cucumber pickle, chopped.	1 tablespoonful seeded raisins.

Way of Preparing:

Brown the flour in the butter, then add the stock and cook five minutes. Season with the salt, paprika, lemon-juice, cucumber pickle, chopped fine and the seeded raisins. Mix thoroughly and serve hot.

CALVES' TONGUE.

Materials:

4 calves' tongues.	2 cups boiling water.
1 onion.	1 tablespoonful vinegar
1 teaspoonful salt.	½ teaspoonful salt.
½ teaspoonful pepper.	¼ teaspoonful paprika.
3 tablespoonfuls flour.	1 tablespoonful capers.
3 tablespoonfuls butter.	12 stoned olives sliced.

Grinding Pillsbury's Best Flour.

Way of Preparing:

Cover the tongues with boiling water, and add the onion, sliced together with one teaspoonful of salt and one-half teaspoonful of pepper. Cover and simmer slowly until thoroughly done. Remove from the water and skin the tongues, and cut them lengthwise in halves. Brown the butter in a saucepan, add the flour and brown thoroughly, stirring carefully all the while, and then add the boiling water. Season with the other one-half teaspoonful of salt, paprika, vinegar and capers. Then add the tongues, which should have been reheated. Dish on a hot platter, add the olives and serve.

Quantity:

This will serve four persons.

CORN BEEF HASH.

Materials:

1 pint chopped cold corned beef.	1 pint cold chopped potatoes.
½ teaspoonful salt.	½ teaspoonful pepper.
¼ cup cream.	1 tablespoonful butter.
	Onion.

Way of Preparing:

Rub the inside of your frying pan with a cut onion. Put in the butter and let it get hot. Then add the meat, potatoes, salt and pepper, having them well mixed. Moisten the whole with the cream, spread evenly and place the pan so that the hash can brown slowly and evenly underneath. When done, fold over and turn out on the platter. You can do the browning in the oven if you prefer.

Quantity:

This will serve four persons.

CREOLE TRIPE.

Materials:

2 pints tripe.	½ cup drained tomatoes.
2 tablespoonfuls butter.	3 fresh mushrooms.
1 onion.	1 teaspoonful salt.
½ green pepper.	Boiled rice.
1 tablespoonful flour.	Parsley chopped.
1 cup boiling water.	

Way of Preparing:

Put the butter in a saucepan and cook in it the onion, chopped fine. Then add the flour, the green pepper finely chopped, the boiling water, the tomatoes, the mushrooms, peeled and sliced and the salt, boil five minutes. Cut the tripe in pieces one and one-half inch square, and press them between folds of cheese cloth, to remove all the moisture. Add the tripe to the contents of the sauce-pan, and simmer ten minutes. Dish on a hot platter, surrounded by a border of boiled rice. Sprinkle with finely chopped parsley and serve.

Quantity:

This will serve five persons.

CURRIED LAMB.

Materials:

4 cups lamb, cut in inch pieces.
1 large onion sliced.
1 quart boiling water.
1 stalk celery.
3 sprigs thyme.
½ teaspoonful pepper.
3 sprigs parsley.

2 tablespoonfuls butter.
2 tablespoonfuls flour.
1 teaspoonful curry powder.
1 teaspoonful salt.
Cold water.
Boiled rice.

Way of Preparing:

Put the lamb in a kettle, cover with cold water, and bring to the boiling point. Pour off the water and rinse the meat in cold water, return it to the kettle and add one quart of boiling water, the onion cut in slices, the thyme and the parsley. Simmer slowly until the meat is tender, then remove it and strain the liquor. Melt the butter in a saucepan and add the flour, then add the curry powder, salt, pepper and strained liquor. Cook three minutes, add the meat; thoroughly reheat and serve with a garniture of boiled rice.

Quantity:

This will serve six persons.

DEVILED STEAK.

Materials:

1 flank steak.
1 large onion.
2 tablespoonfuls butter.
2 tablespoonfuls flour.
1 teaspoonful salt.
½ teaspoonful pepper.

⅛ teaspoonful paprika.
1 teaspoonful mustard.
3 tablespoonfuls vinegar.
2 cups hot water.

Way of Preparing:

Melt the butter in a frying pan, slice the onion and fry it in the butter. Remove the onion when it is brown. Cut the steak in pieces three inches long and two inches wide, dredge them lightly in flour and fry in the butter. Remove the meat from the frying pan and add to the butter the salt, vinegar, mustard, pepper, paprika and the remaining flour. Then add the hot water. Replace the steak in the frying pan, cover closely and allow it to simmer until the steak is tender. Dish on a hot platter, pour the gravy over it, garnish with fried potatoes and serve.

Quantity:

This will serve six persons.

Packing Pillsbury's Best Flour.

FRIED PIGS' FEET.

Materials:

Pigs' feet.
Lemon juice.
Salt and pepper.

Lard and butter.
Batter to taste.

Way of Preparing:

Wash the feet and put them on to boil in cold water. Bring them quickly to the boiling point and then reduce the heat. Allow them to simmer until very tender, then remove them from the kettle, and allow them to get cold. When cold and firm, split them in halves with a sharp knife, season with pepper and salt, dip them in batter and fry in deep fat. Drain on blotting paper and serve very hot. Instead of frying them you may make—

BROILED PIGS' FEET.

by sprinkling them with pepper and salt and broiling them for ten minutes. Dress with butter and lemon juice.

HAMBURG STEAK.

Materials:

2 lbs. round steak.
1 teaspoonful salt.
½ teaspoonful pepper.
½ cup boiling water.

1 teaspoonful onion juice.
1 egg.
½ cup flour.
½ cup drippings.

Way of Preparing:

Chop the meat very fine and add the seasonings. Beat the egg, and mix it with the meat. Divide into four equal portions, and shape into round cakes, about one inch thick. Dredge these on both sides with flour, and fry in the drippings, turning them so as to brown both sides. When nicely browned, add the half-cup of boiling water. Cover closely and simmer for forty-five minutes.

Quantity:

This will serve four persons.

HUNGARIAN GOULASH.

A National Dish ("Gulyas" In Hungarian).

Materials:

3 lbs. veal in inch cubes
3 large potatoes diced.
½ cup water.
1 teaspoonful salt.
3 large onions, sliced.
½ teaspoonful paprika.

1 cup butter or drippings.
1 cup cream.
½ teaspoonful black pepper.

Way of Preparing:

Put the butter or drippings in a kettle on the range, and when hot add the onions and fry them; add the veal and cook until brown. Add the water, cover closely, and cook very slowly until the meat is tender, then add the seasonings and place the po-

tatoes on top of the meat. Cover and cook until
the potatoes are tender, but not falling to pieces.
Then add the cream and cook five minutes longer.

Quantity:

This dish will serve six persons.

PORK TENDERLOIN LARDED.

Materials:

½ lb. fat pork.	2 tablespoonfuls butter.
4 large pork tenderloins.	1 teaspoonful salt.
1 cup cracker crumbs.	½ teaspoonful pepper.
1 cup boiling water.	1 teaspoonful poultry seasoning.

Way of Preparing:

Wipe the tenderloins clean with a damp cloth.
With a sharp knife make a deep pocket lengthwise
in each tenderloin laying the tenderloin flat on the
table and making the incisions along the sides.
Cut your pork into long thin strips, and with a lard-
ing needle lard each tenderloin. Melt the butter in
the water, add the seasonings and the cracker
crumbs, combining all thoroughly. Now fill each
pocket in the tenderloins with this stuffing, sew up
the pockets closely with a coarse thread and needle,
place the tenderloins in a baking pan, and bake in a
brisk oven forty-five minutes basting constantly
with a—

BROWN SAUCE

made of the following

Materials:

2 tablespoonfuls butter.	½ teaspoonful salt.
1 small onion.	¼ teaspoonful pepper.
2 tablespoonfuls flour.	½ bayleaf.
1½ cups boiling water.	

Way of Preparing:

Cook the onion in the butter five minutes. Remove the onion, add the flour, and stir until well
browned. Add the seasonings and the boiling water.
Keep hot and baste your tenderloins with it. When
the tenderloins are done, serve them on a hot platter and pour around them any remaining sauce.

Quantity:

This will serve eight persons.

POT ROAST BEEF.

Materials:

5 lbs. beef.	1 carrot, chopped fine.
½ lb. suet.	1 tablespoonful flour.
6 cloves.	1 pint boiling water.
2 bayleaves.	Salt and pepper.
2 slices onion.	

Way of Preparing:

Put the suet in a kettle and add the onion, bay-leaves, cloves and chopped carrot; let it cook five minutes and get very hot. Put in the meat, well seasoned with salt and pepper and brown it on both sides. Add the water, cover closely and simmer until very tender. Remove from the pot and thicken the liquor remaining in the pot with the flour. Strain and serve it in a sauceboat.

Note—As the roast cooks, add boiling water to keep the quantity the same as at first.

Quantity:

This will serve eight persons.

SPANISH HASH.

Materials.

1 cup cold roast meat (any kind).	Tabasco sauce, pepper and salt.
4 cold boiled potatoes.	1 green pepper.
2 small onions.	1 egg.
	1 cup tomatoes, canned.

Way of Preparing:

Chop together your cold potatoes, onions and green pepper, then add one cup chopped cold roast meat and one of tomatoes. Season with pepper and salt, and three drops of tabasco sauce; then add the egg, well beaten. Drop by spoonfuls into your muffin-rings. Bake in a hot oven and serve with tomato sauce.

SCALLOPED BRAINS.

Materials:

Calves' brains.	Salt and pepper.
Bread crumbs.	Butter.
Milk.	

Way of Preparing:

Soak the brains in cold water one hour. Parboil in salted water ten minutes. Remove the skins. Grease a baking dish and put in a layer of the brains, sliced. Then put on a layer of crumbs, sprinkle with salt and pepper and dot with butter. Now add another layer of brains, then another one of crumbs, salt and pepper and butter, alternating in this way until the dish is nearly full. Fill with milk and bake three quarters of an hour in a moderate oven.

STUFFED HAM.

Materials:

1 medium sized ham.	1 teaspoonful allspice.
1 pint bread crumbs.	1 teaspoonful cinnamon
1 teaspoonful mustard.	1 teaspoonful black
3 eggs, well beaten.	pepper.
1 teaspoonful red pepper.	1 tablespoonful chopped celery.
1 cup brown sugar.	1 cup sweet milk.
3 pickles, chopped.	Boiled eggs.
1 teaspoonful cloves	Cloves.

Way of Preparing:

Boil the ham for three hours; after it is cold skin it and make incisions in the ham, one inch apart from each other, lengthwise, and as deep as possible.

Make a stuffing of the bread crumbs and a teaspoonful each of mustard, cloves, cinnamon, allspice, three well-beaten eggs, black and red pepper mixed, the chopped celery, brown sugar, the chopped pickles and the sweet milk. Mix these ingredients thoroughly into a soft paste, fill the incisions and cover the ham with the same.

Put in the oven and brown slowly. Garnish the ham, when done, with slices of boiled egg and pickles, sticking a whole clove into each piece of pickle.

SWEETBREADS, GOMEZ STYLE.

A Cuban Dish.

Materials:

4 beef sweetbreads.	2 tablespoonfuls flour.
2 large oranges.	½ teaspoonful pepper.
1 lemon, medium.	1 egg.
1 cup butter.	1 green pepper.
1 cup boiling water.	Parsley.
1 teaspoonful salt.	

Way of Preparing:

Parboil the sweetbreads until tender, plunge them into cold water, drain and with a sharp knife trim the sweetbreads, removing the skin and gristly membrane. Sprinkle them with the juice of one orange and place in an ice box for two hours. At the end of that time place them in a baking pan, dredge with flour, sprinkle with salt and pepper, dot with butter and pour over them half a cup of boiling water. Then add the orange juice in which they stood in the ice box and the green pepper, cut in thin strips. Place in the oven and cook until nicely brown, basting them frequently, serve with a

CUBAN GRAVY

made as follows: Cream one-half a cup of butter. Mix one-fourth teaspoonful of salt, one eighth teaspoonful of paprika, the juice of one-half of an orange, the juice of one lemon, one-half a cup of boiling water. To this add one egg, well beaten, and cook in a double boiler until thick and smooth. Add the creamed butter, pour around your sweetbreads, and serve garnished with parsley and slices of orange.

Quantity:

This will serve six persons.

VEAL LOAF.

Materials:

3 lbs. lean veal.	1 teaspoonful salt.
½ lb. raw ham.	1 teaspoonful pepper.
3 eggs, well beaten.	3 tablespoonfuls cream.
3 soda crackers, rolled fine.	2 tablespoonfuls boiling water.

Way of Preparing:

Chop the veal and ham very fine, then add the salt and pepper, the cracker crumbs, the well beaten eggs, the cream and the hot water. Mix all these together very thoroughly, grease a bread-pan perfectly and pack the mixture into it, pressing it down firmly. Cover and bake in a moderate oven one hour. Uncover and bake half an hour longer. Serve either hot or cold in slices.

Quantity:

This will serve eight persons.

PASTRY & PIES

Pies are one of the few specifically national American dishes. The digestibility of pies has been called into question. Properly made pies are as digestible as anything else.

Paste for pies should be quite thin and rolled a little larger than the tin to allow for shrinkage. Allow more paste for the upper than the under crust, and be sure to perforate the former. Always brush the under crust with cold water and press the upper one down on it. When bak ing a juicy fruit pie make an incision in the center and place a small funnel-shaped piece of paper into the incision. This will keep the juice from escaping at the sides of the pie. Never grease a pie tin. Properly made pastry will grease its own tin. For baking, pastry requires from thirty to forty-five minutes.

APPLE PIE.

Materials:

Apples.	Pie Paste.
Sugar.	Cinnamon.
Water.	Butter.

Way of Preparing:

Line a deep pie tin with rich paste, select large tart apples. Pare and quarter and cut each quarter into four pieces. Put an even layer of these pieces in the prepared tin, sprinkle with sugar, dot with butter, dust with cinnamon and bake in a moderate oven for forty-five minutes.

Three tablespoons of prepared tea are sometimes used instead of the water for moistening.

Quantity:

This will serve four or six.

CHERRY PIE.

Materials:

1 quart cherries.   1 tablespoonful flour.
1 cup sugar.   Pastry.

Way of Preparing:

Stem and pit the cherries, sift the flour and sugar together and add to the cherries. Line a pie tin with rich pastry. Put in the prepared cherries, cover with pastry, and bake in a moderate oven for thirty-five minutes.

Quantity:

Serve four or six persons.

CHEESE PIE.

Materials:

4 eggs.   1 lemon.
1 lb. cottage cheese.   1½ cups sugar.

Way of Preparing:

Beat the whites and yolks of the eggs separately. To the beaten yolks add the sugar, beating thoroughly, then add the grated rind and the juice of the lemon. Pass the cheese through a colander, and then add it, beating again thoroughly. Lastly stir in the beaten whites. Line a pie tin with raw pie crust, pour in the mixture and bake in a moderate oven.

Quantity:

This will serve four or six persons.

CREAM PUFFS.

Materials:

1 cup flour.   ½ lb. butter.
¾ cup water.   5 eggs.
Pinch salt.   Filling.

Way of Preparing:

Heat the water and add the butter and salt. When this boils stir in the flour. Take care to have no lumps. Cook until the mixture leaves the side of the saucepan. Pour out and allow it to cool. When nearly cold add the unbeaten eggs, one at a time. Mix in each one thoroughly before adding the next. After adding all cover the mixture and let it stand for one hour. When ready to bake, drop it by the spoonful on buttered tins leaving space for them to rise. Bake in a moderate oven for forty-five minutes. They should feel dry and crisp to the touch. When cold, split and fill with whipped cream. If desired they can be fried in deep fat, like doughnuts. If you intend frying them use only a teaspoonful at a time.

Quantity:

Makes eighteen Cream Puffs.

THIS PHOTOGRAPH shows the relative position of the mills to the great St. Anthony's Falls water-power, and fixes at a glance the immense advantage of mills thus located; in addition to this advantage, there are other advantages possessed by Minneapolis, as a flour milling center.

Minneapolis lies at the very gates of the greatest wheat fields in the world; not greatest in amount alone, but these fields grow the best wheat now known to modern scientific millers.

It requires more than 130,000 bushels of wheat per day for use in making PILLSBURY'S BEST flour, or more than one-third of the entire receipts

of Minneapolis. According to our standard, this one-third must be the best of the wheat.

It is a matter of note among millers visiting our mills that PILLSBURY'S are not only the largest but best equipped and up-to-date mills. Higher salaries are paid to PILLSBURY millers and mill workers, taken as a whole from bottom to top than any millers. Naturally the very best talent is drawn.

This combination of great power, convenient location next to the wheat fields, best equipped mills, most skilled and intelligent workmen, are the main reasons why PILLSBURY'S BEST is the best and must continue so to be.

CUSTARD PIE.

Materials:

4 eggs.   4 heaping tablespoon-
1 pint sweet milk.   fuls sugar.
1 heaping tablespoonful Flavoring extract.
flour.

Way of Preparing:

Beat the eggs just enough to blend thoroughly, then add the sugar, then the flour and lastly the milk.

Flavor to taste and bake in a raw crust until the custard is set.

Quantity:

This. will serve four or six persons.

DULING APPLE DUMPLINGS.

Materials:

2 cups flour.   ⅞ cup sweet milk.
2 teaspoonfuls baking   1 teaspoonful cinnamon
powder.   2 tablespoonfuls brown
1 teaspoonful salt.   sugar.
1 tablespoonful butter.   3 tart apples, chopped.
1 tablespoonful lard.

Way of Preparing:

Sift the flour, baking powder and salt. Work into these the butter and lard. Then make a dough, using the milk. Place on your molding board. Roll out into a sheet one-half an inch thick. Brush with melted butter and sprinkle with the brown sugar and cinnamon. Then cover with the chopped apples. Roll it up, as you would a jelly roll, and cut into twelve equal slices. Place the slices on end in a buttered pan. Pour over them the sauce and bake in a brisk oven for twenty-five minutes. Following is the—

DUMPLING SAUCE.

Materials:

1 cup sugar.   ½ teaspoonful salt.
1 tablespoonful butter.   1 cup hot water.
1 tablespoonful flour.   ½ lemon, sliced.

Way of Preparing:

Mix the sugar, flour and salt. Add butter, sliced lemon and hot water. Stir until well mixed. Cook three minutes, and then pour it over the raw dumplings.

Quantity:

This will serve 12 people.

EGG KISSES.

Materials:

Whites of 4 eggs.   1¼ cups powdered sugar
1 teaspoonful vanilla.

Way of Preparing:

Beat the whites of the eggs until they are stiff. Gradually add two-thirds of the sugar and continue beating until the mixture will hold its shape. Fold in the remaining sugar and flavor. Shape with a spoon on a board covered with letter paper. Bake very slowly for thirty minutes, remove from the paper and put together in pairs.

If you wish to fill them with ice cream, first remove the inner soft part and place in the oven to dry.

GRANDMOTHER'S PIE.

Materials:

5 eggs.
1 cup sugar.

The grated rind and juice of two lemons.
Pastry.

Way of Preparing:

Beat the eggs, add the sugar, then the rind and juice of the lemons. Bake in a small tart-pan, lined with rich crust.

Quantity:

This will serve four persons.

LEMON CREAM PIE.

Materials:

4 eggs.
1 cup sugar.
2 heaping tablespoonfuls flour.

1½ cups boiling water.
The grated rind and juice of two lemons.

Way of Preparing:

Beat the yolks and whites of the eggs separately. To the beaten yolks add the sugar, flour, lemon juice and rind, and lastly the boiling water. Cook in a double boiler and when it begins to thicken, add to it one-half of the beaten whites. Stir this in thoroughly and let it cook until it is as thick as desired.

Use the remainder of the whites for the meringue on top of the pie. After your custard has cooled, fill a baked shell, pile the meringue on top, and bake in a very slow oven until the meringue is brown.

Quantity:

This will serve four or six persons.

MINCE PIE.

Materials:

4 lbs. beef tenderloin or tongue.
3 lbs. suet.
3 lbs. brown sugar.
3 lbs. seeded raisins.
3 lbs. currants.
1 oz. mace.
1 oz. nutmeg.
1 oz. cinnamon.
1 oz. cloves.

10 large apples, chopped fine.
2 lbs. citron, sliced.
Grated rind and juice of four lemons.
Juice and grated rind of four oranges.
1 quart brandy.
1 pint Madeira wine.
1 tablespoonful salt.

Way of Preparing:

Boil the beef very well done, and chop it fine. Chop suet and apples and add to the beef. Mix the sugar, mace, nutmeg, cinnamon and cloves and add to them the wine, brandy, lemon juice and orange juice.

Mix the raisins, currants, citron and lemon and orange rinds.

Now combine gradually the three sets of ingredients, after having added the salt to the liquid part, using a portion of each until all are used.

Pack in stone jars, cover closely and keep in a dry cool closet.

Quantity:

This will make enough to last all winter.

PLAIN PIE CRUSTS.

Materials:

1¼ cups Pillsbury's Best.
1 level teaspoonful salt.
1 level teaspoonful baking powder.
1 heaping tablespoonful butter.
1 heaping tablespoonful lard.
2 tablespoonfuls ice water.

Way of Preparing:

Have all material as cold as possible. Cream the butter and lard together, and add the salt. Sift the flour and baking powder and work into them thoroughly the creamed butter and lard. Reserve one heaping tablespoonful of this dry mixture. Take the two tablespoonfuls of ice water and make a dough. If this is not enough wetting, add a very small quantity of ice water.

Roll this dough out thin and sprinkle over it the dry mixture.

Fold it over from each side and roll again. It is now ready for use.

Quantity:

Enough for one large covered pie or two shells.

PUFF PASTE.

Materials:

1 lb. butter.
1 lb. pastry flour.
Ice water.

Way of Preparing:

Wash the butter and remove all the water. Reserve two tablespoonfuls of it and shape the remainder into a round cake one-half inch thick. Place it on a floured pastry board. Work the two tablespoons of butter into the flour. Make a dough with ice water. Turn on a board and knead for two minutes. Cover and let stand for ten minutes. Roll out one-quarter inch thick, keeping the paste oblong and square at the corners.

Place the cake of butter on the lower half of the cake of paste, and fold the other half over the butter. Press down the edges firmly. Fold the right side of the paste over the enclosed butter and the left side under it. Turn the paste half way around, and let it stand ten minutes. Roll out having the paste oblong. Fold from the ends towards the center, making three layers. Cover and let stand ten minutes. Repeat this three times, turning the paste halfway around each time. After the fifth rolling, fold the ends toward the center and double over. Chill but do not let it come in touch with the ice. Bake on a tin covered with a double thickness of brown paper.

PUMPKIN PIE.

Materials:

3 eggs.	1 teaspoonful cinnamon
1 cup sugar.	½ teaspoonful allspice.
1 cup stewed pumpkin.	½ teaspoonful cloves.
1 teaspoonful ginger.	1 pint milk.

Way of Preparing:

Beat the eggs, add to them the sugar, the pumpkin and the spices. Beat it thoroughly and then add the milk and mix thoroughly, then bake in a raw crust.

Quantity:

This will serve four or six persons.

SQUASH PIE No. 1.

Materials:

2 cups prepared squash	1 cup milk.
½ cup sugar.	½ teaspoonful cinnamon
2 eggs.	½ teaspoonful ginger.
1 tablespoonful flour.	¼ teaspoonful salt.

Way of Preparing:

Beat the eggs and add the sugar, then the squash, salt and spices. After that add the flour and lastly, add the milk gradually. Line a pie plate with pastry and pour on it the mixture. Bake for five minutes in a brisk oven.

Reduce the heat and bake slowly until the custard is set.

You can make a

SWEET POTATO PIE.

in precisely the same way, substituting sweet potatoes in the place of squash.

Quantity:

This will serve four or six persons.

SQUASH PIE No. 2.

Materials:

1½ cups squash.	½ teaspoonful salt.
1-3 cup sugar.	¼ teaspoonful nutmeg.
1 egg.	¼ teaspoonful cinnamon
1 cup milk.	1 tablespoonful melted butter.

Way of Preparing:

Steam and strain squash to make 1½ cups. Add sugar, salt, spice, butter, egg slightly beaten, and milk gradually.

After the crust is set, bake slowly.

If a richer pie is desired, omit butter, take new milk, or half milk and half cream, and use one more egg yolk.

Quantity:

This makes one large pie.

WHITE MINCE MEAT.

Materials:

1 turkey, roasted.	1 lb. citron, sliced.
2 lbs. roast veal.	1 lb. almonds, shredded
2 lbs. chopped suet.	1 lb. preserved ginger, chopped.
6 chopped apples.	½ pint white wine.
1 lb. white sugar.	Juice of 3 oranges.
1 pint brandy.	
2 cocoanuts.	

Way of Preparing:

Mince the turkey meat very fine, and add the veal, chopped, and the suet. Mix well and add the apples, cocoanut, citron, almonds and ginger. Mix the sugar, brandy, wine and orange juice and pour over the other mixture. Mix thoroughly and pack in stone jars. Cover closely and keep in a cool dry place.

Quantity:

This will make six quarts.

POULTRY

CHICKEN CROQUETTES.

Materials:

1 pint cold cooked chicken.
½ pint milk.
1 heaping tablespoonful butter.
2 tablespoonfuls flour.
1 teaspoonful onion juice.
1 teaspoonful salt.
¼ teaspoonful nutmeg.
½ teaspoonful pepper.
Flour, beaten eggs, cracker crumbs, lard

Way of Preparing:

Chop the meat very fine. Heat the milk in a double boiler. Cream the butter, and flour and add it to the milk, then add the onion juice and seasonings. Cook until you have a thick sauce. Pour this over the chopped chicken, and mix thoroughly then let it cool, and form into shapes. Flour lightly, dip shapes into the beaten eggs, roll in cracker crumbs, and fry in deep fat.

Quantity:

This will serve six persons.

CHICKEN EN CASSEROLE.

(Casserole is the French for an earthen, covered dish.)

Materials:

2½ lbs. chicken.
1 can mushrooms.
1 carrot.
1 onion.
1 tablespoonful chopped parsley.
1 teaspoonful salt.
½ teaspoonful pepper.
1 tablespoonful flour.
2 cups boiling water.
1 stalk celery.
½ cup of butter.

Way of Preparing:

Clean and dress the chicken and steam it until tender. Melt the butter in a frying pan, add all the vegetables, chopped fine, cook five minutes and then add the flour. Add all the seasonings to the hot water, pour it into the frying pan and let it cook five minutes. Put the chicken in a casserole, dredge with flour, dust with salt and pepper, and pour the contents of the frying pan over it. Place it in the oven and cook until the chicken is thoroughly browned. Remove from the oven, cover the dish and serve in the casserole.

Quantity:

This will serve five persons.

FRIED SPRING CHICKEN.
Southern Style.

Materials:

1 chicken.	1 cup lard.
½ cup flour.	Pepper and salt.

Way of Preparing:

Select a large plump spring chicken, kill, scald and pluck. Draw and cut into the natural joints. Then put them into icewater for five minutes. Drain and place on a platter in the ice box for two hours. Dredge thickly with flour and sprinkle with salt and pepper. Place the lard in a frying pan and when it is hot saute the chicken in it, taking care to turn it often so it will not burn, but cook thoroughly, serve with cream gravy.

Some prefer frying bacon enough with the chicken to make the required amount of fat. If you do so, serve some of the bacon with the chicken.

POTATO STUFFING.
For Fowl.

Materials:

2 cups hot, mashed potatoes.	¼ cup butter.
1 cup crumbs.	1 teaspoonful salt.
¼ cup salt pork, chopped	½ teaspoonful sage.
1 teaspoonful onion juice.	1 egg.

Way of Preparing:

Add to the potatoes the butter, egg, salt, onion juice, sage, crumbs, and pork, mix thoroughly and use as stuffing.

ROAST GOOSE.

Materials:

1 large goose.	Pepper.
6 strips salt pork.	Stuffing.
1 cup water.	Apple sauce.
Salt.	Watercress.

Way of Preparing:

Scrub the goose with hot soap suds, then draw, wash thoroughly in cold water and wipe dry. Stuff, truss, sprinkle with salt and pepper and cover the entire breast with the strips of salt pork. Place on the rack in the dripping pan, pour the water into the latter under the goose. Place in a hot oven and bake for two hours and a half, basting every ten minutes. Remove the pork the last half hour. Garnish the dish with water cress and serve with apple sauce.

The recipe for stuffing made of potatoes is given herein.

SPANISH STEW.

Materials:

3½ lbs. chicken.	1 teaspoonful salt.
5 ripe tomatoes.	1 quart boiling water.
4 red peppers.	1 onion.
1 can French peas.	Boiled rice or mashed
1 can mushrooms.	potatoes.
3 large potatoes.	

Way of Preparing:

Clean and joint the chicken, slice the tomatoes, shred the peppers (removing seeds) and slice the onions. Place the chicken in a kettle with the tomatoes, peppers and onions. Add the boiling water. Cover the kettle and simmer until the chicken is tender, then remove the chicken, strain what remains in the kettle and rub the vegetable part through a sieve. Return vegetables to the kettle and add one can of French peas, a can of mushrooms, and the potatoes, grated, also the salt and cook until the potatoes are tender. Then replace the chicken in the kettle and heat thoroughly.

Serve with a border of mashed potatoes or boiled rice.

Quantity:

This will serve eight persons.

PUDDINGS

The proof of the pudding is the eating.
—Cervantes.

BREAD PUDDING.

Materials:

1 pint bread crumbs.
3 cups milk.
½ cup sugar.
¼ cup butter.

3 eggs.
1 teaspoonful vanilla.
½ teaspoonful salt.
1 cup chopped citron.

Way of Preparing:

Heat the milk and pour over the crumbs. Cream the butter and sugar and add the eggs, salt and vanilla. When the milk is cold combine the two mixtures and add the chopped citron. Pour into a buttered pudding dish and bake forty minutes. Serve with any desired sauce.

Quantity:

This will serve six persons.

FROZEN PUDDING.

Materials:

1 pint milk.
Scant ½ cup flour.
2 tablespoonfuls gelatine.
1 lb French candied fruits (½ lb. will do)

2 cups sugar.
2 eggs.
1 quart cream.
4 tablespoonfuls wine.

Way of Preparing:

Let the milk come to a boil. Beat the flour, one cup of sugar and the eggs together and stir into the boiling milk. Cook 20 minutes and then add your gelatine after soaking one or two hours. Set away to cool. When cool, add the wine, one cup of sugar and the cream. Freeze ten minutes, then add the fruit and finish freezing. Take out the beater, pack smoothly and set away for an hour or two.

Quantity:

This will serve six or eight persons.

HOT SNOW BALLS.

Materials:

3 cups pastry flour.
1 cup confectioners' XXXX sugar.
½ cup butter.
½ cup milk.
Whites of 6 eggs.
3 teaspoonfuls baking powder.

Way of Preparing:

Cream the butter and add the sugar. Beat for five minutes. Sift the flour and baking powder and add to the former alternating with the milk. Lastly fold in the stiffly-beaten whites of the eggs. Fill buttered cups half full and steam for thirty minutes. Serve with orange marmalade and whipped cream or with your favorite sauce.

Quantity:

This will serve twelve persons.

MACAROON PUDDING.

Materials:

½ lb. macaroons.
2 eggs.
¼ teaspoonful salt.
1 cup cream.
¼ teaspoonful almond extract.
Sherry wine.
5 tablespoonfuls sugar.
1 cup milk.
2 tablespoonfuls almonds, blanched and chopped.

Way of Preparing:

Soak a dozen macaroons ten minutes in sherry wine and then remove them. Beat two eggs slightly and add the sugar, salt, milk and the cream, then add the chopped almonds, the almond extract and four finely-powdered macaroons. Turn this mixture into a pudding dish, arrange your soaked macaroons on top, cover and bake thirty minutes in a hot oven.

Quantity:

This will serve six persons.

PINEAPPLE PUDDING.

Materials:

1 can pineapple.
1 small tea cup sugar.
½ pint whipped cream
½ box gelatine, or 2½ tablespoonfuls granulated gelatine.

Way of Preparing:

Pour juice off of pineapple. Dissolve gelatine in half a pint of hot water. Chop pineapple very fine and mix with sugar. Add this to the dissolved gelatine. When this begins to stiffen, stir in the whipped cream, beating thoroughly.
Set in a cool place to harden.

Quantity:

Will serve six.

PLUM PUDDING.

Materials:

½ lb. bread crumbs.
½ lb. suet, chopped.
½ lb. sugar.
4 eggs.
½ lb. seeded raisins.
½ lb. currants.
½ lb. figs, chopped.
1 cup milk.

¼ lb. citron, sliced.
½ cup brandy.
1 teaspoonful nutmeg.
½ teaspoonful cinnamon
½ teaspoonful cloves.
¼ teaspoonful mace.
1 teaspoonful salt.

Way of Preparing:

Scald the milk and pour it over the crumbs, cream the suet, and add the sugar and the well-beaten yolks of the eggs. When milk and crumbs are cool, combine them with the other mixture, and add the raisins, figs, currants, citron, salt and spices.

Then add the brandy, and lastly, the stiffly-beaten whites of the eggs. Pour into a buttered mold and steam five hours, serve with hard sauce or brandy sauce.

Quantity:

This will make one large or two small puddings.

RICE PUDDING.

Materials:

2 cups boiled rice.
1 pint milk.
4 eggs.
¾ cup sugar.

1 tablespoonful flour.
1 teaspoonful lemon
extract.

Way of Preparing:

Slightly beat the eggs. Add the sugar and flour and mix with the rice. Then add the flavoring and lastly the milk. Bake in a moderate oven until set. Serve with whipped cream or sauce.

This can be made very rich by spreading on top a layer of orange marmalade and covering it with a meringue.

Quantity:

This will serve six persons.

RUSSIAN CREAM.

Materials:

1-3 box gelatine.
1 pint milk.
1 teaspoonful vanilla.

4 eggs.
½ cup sugar.
Hot water.

Way of Preparing:

Dissolve the gelatine in hot water. Beat the yolks of the eggs separately with the sugar. Stir in the milk and make into a custard in a double boiler. Before removing from the range stir in the dissolved gelatine and the vanilla. Beat the whites of the eggs to a stiff froth, strain the custard into them, and then stir all together. Pour into small molds and set away to serve cold.

Quantity:

This will serve six persons.

SPANISH CREAM.

Materials:

1-3 box gelatine, or 1½ tablespoonfuls of granulated gelatine.	1 pint milk.
	3 eggs.
	4 tablespoonfuls sugar.
4 tablespoonfuls cold water.	1 tablespoonful vanilla.

Way of Preparing:

Soak gelatine in 4 tablespoonfuls cold water. When dissolved put it with the milk in a double boiler. Add the sugar to the yolks of eggs and beat till very light. Turn into the hot milk and stir, as for a soft custard. Take from range, and add the well-beaten whites of eggs, and the vanilla. Turn into a mold to harden, and set in a cold place. This is best made several hours before serving. It may be varied by adding sliced peaches, oranges or strawberries, and more sugar, according to fruit.

Quantity:

Will serve six.

SUET PUDDING.

Materials:

1 cup suet.	1 cup molasses.
1 cup sour milk.	3 cups flour.
2 eggs.	½ cup sugar.
1 teaspoonful soda.	1 teaspoonful ginger.
½ teaspoonful salt.	½ teaspoonful cloves.
½ teaspoonful grated nutmeg.	½ teaspoonful cinnamon

Way of Preparing:

Beat the eggs and add the sugar, then the suet, chopped very fine, then the molasses, and after it the flour. Dissolve the soda in the sour milk and add it to the mixture, lastly add the spices.

Pour into a buttered mold and steam three hours.

Quantity:

This will make one large or two small puddings.

SALADS

For a very long time the French nation held first place as the home of salads, now America has become the land of salads, for the simple but very good reason that the greater variety of fruits and vegetables obtainable the year round enables us to assume the position once held by France.

As a nation we eat too few green salads and too many sweet ones. We should cultivate a taste for wholesome green foods. No absolute rules can be laid down for the making of salads, but as the simpler ones are always acceptable, begin with them and you will gradually become an expert saladmaker. The one rule applying to all salads is to have them very cold and to serve them daintily. A few of those liked most will be found herein. You can invent many others, for salads are nowadays made of everything imaginable.

AMBROSIA SALAD.

Materials:

1 pineapple.	1 quart grated cocoanut
1 pint strawberries.	6 oranges.
4 bananas.	Sugar.
1 cup sherry wine.	

Way of Preparing:

Peel and slice the pineapple and cut the slices into thin strips. Hull the berries and cut in halves. Peel the oranges and divide into their natural divisions. Cut these in halves, sprinkle all these ingredients with sugar and put them on ice.

When ready to serve, sprinkle the bottom of a deep salad bowl with the grated cocoanut, then put in the pineapple and again some cocoanut, after that the strawberries, oranges and bananas, putting a layer of cocoanut between each two layers of fruit with a layer of cocoanut on top.

Pour over all the sherry, combined with the juices that have drained from the different fruits.

Garnish with whole strawberries, and thin slices of orange, reserved from the original materials and serve in punch cups.

Have it very cold.

Quantity:

This will serve ten persons.

CHERRY SALAD.

Materials:

1 lb. large California cherries.	1 head lettuce.
½ lb. shelled hazel nuts.	10 tablespoonfuls sugar.
2 tablespoonfuls Maraschino.	½ cup sherry wine.
	2 tablespoonfuls orange juice.

Way of Preparing:

Stone the cherries and replace each stone with a blanched hazel nut. Line the salad bowl with the lettuce. Sprinkle the cherries with the sugar and pour over them a dressing made of the orange juice, sherry and maraschino.

Garnish the dish with bunches of cherries and cherry blossoms if possible.

Quantity:

This will serve six persons.

CHICKEN SALAD.

Materials:

1 chicken.	Lemon juice.
1 onion, sliced.	Celery.
1 bay leaf.	Mayonnaise.
6 cloves.	Whipped cream.
1 teaspoonful salt.	Lettuce.
½ teaspoonful white pepper.	Mace.
	Capers.

Way of Preparing:

Clean and dress the chicken. Place in boiling water, add the onion, bay leaf, cloves and mace. Bring to a boil and let it boil rapidly for five minutes. Reduce the heat to below the boiling point, and let it cook until tender.

By cooking it in this manner the dark meat will be almost as white as the meat of the breast. When the chicken is cold, cut into half-inch cubes, removing all the fat and skin. To each pint allow one tablespoonful lemon juice, sprinkle the latter over the prepared chicken and place on ice. When ready to serve, mix the chicken with two-thirds as much white celery cut into corresponding pieces. Dust with salt and pepper, mix the mayonnaise—recipe elsewhere herein—with whipped cream to taste, and pour over the salad. Serve on lettuce leaves and garnish the dish with the white leaves of the celery. Then sprinkle the top of the salad with capers.

Duck, turkey or sweetbreads may be substituted for the chicken and give you—

DUCK SALAD,

TURKEY SALAD and

SWEETBREAD SALAD.

BOILED SALAD DRESSING.

Materials:

3 tablespoonfuls butter.	1 teaspoonful mixed mustard.
6 tablespoonfuls vinegar.	½ teaspoonful salt.
3 eggs.	½ teaspoonful celery salt.
6 tablespoonfuls milk.	¼ teaspoonful pepper.

Way of Preparing:

Put vinegar and butter into porcelain or granite pan, and place on the range. When butter is melted, take off and cool. Beat the eggs until light, add the mustard, salt, celery salt, pepper and milk. Pour this into the cooled mixture, set on range, stirring constantly from the bottom of the pan. When it begins to thicken, take off at once, and stir until smooth.

COOKED SALAD DRESSING.

Materials:

Yolks of 7 eggs.	1 teaspoonful salt.
1 cup hot vinegar.	1 teaspoonful mustard.
2 cups sweet milk.	½ teaspoonful white pepper.
2 tablespoonfuls flour.	
2 tablespoonfuls sugar.	1 tablespoonful butter.

Way of Preparing:

Beat the yolks and add the sugar, salt, mustard, pepper and flour. Mix well and then add the milk slowly. Then add the hot vinegar. Cook in a double boiler until as thick as very thick cream. Remove from the fire and add the butter. Stir until the butter is all melted and thoroughly mixed.

If a milder dressing is desired add half a cup of thick cream to this mixture.

Quantity:

This will make one quart of dressing and you may bottle it while hot and keep until needed.

CUPID SALAD.

Way of Preparing:

4 oranges.

2 bananas.

1-3 cup sugar.

1 pint strawberries.

1 large tart apple.

1 egg.

1 tablespoonful brandy.

Materials:

Cut the oranges in halves, scoop out the pulp, keeping the peel intact. Slice the bananas, and hull and slice the strawberries. Place all materials on ice. Make a dressing of the apple, egg, sugar and brandy. Grate the apple and sprinkle it with sugar as you grate so as to keep it from turning dark, add to it the brandy and unbeaten white of the egg, and with a wire egg-beater beat until it is stiff and fluffy. Take the orange cups and with a pair of sharp scissors cut small scallops near the top and tie them together in pairs, using baby ribbon for tying.

When ready to serve fill the orange cups with the prepared fruit, and heap the dressing on top.

Top off each half orange with a large strawberry.

This is a pretty and significant salad to serve at a luncheon, where there are several young couples.

Place a pair of the cups on a salad plate on the table between each couple.

They can untie them or not, as they please.

Quantity:

This will serve four couples.

ENGLISH WALNUT SALAD.

Materials:

1 pint walnuts.

1 cup minced celery.

Lemon juice.

1 cup chopped apple.

1 tablespoonful olive oil.

Mayonnaise.

Lettuce.

Way of Preparing:

Soak the walnuts in lemon juice for one hour, drain, break into pieces and mix with the celery and apple. Pour over all the olive oil and place on ice for two hours. When ready to serve, place in a salad bowl lined with lettuce leaves and dress with mayonnaise. Garnish with the white leaves of the celery.

FRENCH SALAD DRESSING.

Materials:

3 tablespoonfuls olive oil.

1 tablespoonful vinegar

½ teaspoonful onion juice.

½ teaspoonful salt.

¼ teaspoonful pepper.

Way of Preparing:

Add the salt, pepper and onion juice to the vinegar. Mix with the oil quickly and pour over the salad.

This is the most popular of all salad dressing.

English Salad Dressing.

Is made by the addition of a teaspoonful of made mustard to the given quantity of French Salad Dressing.

FRUIT SALAD.

Materials:

2 doz. English walnuts
2 doz. white grapes.
2 large oranges.
1 pineapple.
3 bananas.
½ cup Madeira wine.

1 cup sugar.
2 tablespoonfuls lemon juice.
½ cup orange juice.
Maraschino cherries.

Way of Preparing:

Blanch the walnut meats and break them into pieces. Skin and seed the grapes. Cut the pineapple after peeling it, into half-inch cubes. Peel and slice the bananas. Peel the oranges, separate the sections, and remove the skin.

Arrange prettily on a salad dish and pour over it a dressing of—

½ cup Madeira wine.
1 cup of sugar.
2 tablespoonfuls lemon juice.

½ cup of orange juice well combined.

Garnish the whole with maraschino cherries.

Quantity:

This will serve six persons.

MACARONI AND CELERY SALAD.

Materials:

1 pint boiled macaroni.
1 pint celery.
½ pint chopped nuts.

½ pint salad dressing.
6 lettuce leaves.

Way of Preparing:

Cut the macaroni into one-half inch pieces. Cut the celery in the same manner and then mix the two.

Then add the salad dressing and sprinkle in the nuts. Line the salad dish with the lettuce leaves. Place the salad on the lettuce in the dish. Chill and serve.

Quantity:

This will serve eight persons.

MAYONNAISE.

Materials:

2 raw egg yolks.
½ pint olive oil.
1 teaspoonful made mustard.
1 teaspoonful lemon juice.

Yolks of 2 boiled eggs.
2 teaspoonfuls salt.
½ teaspoonful pepper.
2 tablespoonfuls vinegar.
Sugar.

Way of Preparing:

Place your mixing bowl in a larger one full of cracked ice. Place the yolk of both raw and boiled eggs in the bowl. Drop in a little oil and rub to a cream. Add the mustard, salt, pepper and a pinch of sugar. Now add the oil, drop by drop, beating all the time until the mixture is thick and stiff enough to keep its shape and has a shiny appearance. Now thin it by addition of the vinegar, a drop at a time, until the dressing is of the proper consistency. Then add the lemon juice, and just before using add the stiffly-beaten whites of the eggs.

Keep this dressing very cold.

If a mild dressing is wanted, omit the mustard and pepper. For a fruit salad omit the mustard and use the sugar instead.

For a still milder dressing omit mustard and pepper, use only half the oil, and use cream instead of the omitted oil.

PINEAPPLE SALAD.

Materials:

1 pineapple.	½ cup sherry wine.
1 pint strawberries.	½ cup orange juice.
2 oranges.	Parsley.
1 cup sugar.	

Way of Preparing:

Select a large pineapple with a straight, nice, green top. Strip off all the leaves leaving the bud in the center. Reserve twelve of the nicest leaves. With a sharp knife cut off the top of the pineapple two inches down, leaving the center bud intact. Then take a fork and pick out all the pulps, leaving the outer wall intact. When finished you have made a nice pineapple bowl. Place this on ice. Hull the strawberries and cut in halves, reserving eighteen of the largest and nicest. Peel the oranges and cut into one-half inch cubes.

Pick the pineapple pulp into shreds and sprinkle with sugar. Place all the materials on ice for some time before serving.

When ready to serve place the twelve pineapple-top leaves in an even circle on a flat round platter, points outward. Set the pineapple bowl in the center. Fill it with alternate layers of pineapple, orange and strawberries. Mix the sherry, orange juice and half the sugar and pour over the fruit in the bowl.

Place a row of halved strawberries, flat side down, around the edge of the top of the pineapple bowl and then put on the top of the pineapple. Make a wreath around the bottom with the reserved eighteen strawberries and the parsley.

Quantity:

This will serve six persons.

POTATO SALAD.

Materials:

6 boiled potatoes, sliced while hot and allowed to cool.
1 small onion, minced fine.
½ teaspoonful salt.
2 tablespoonfuls minced celery.
tablespoonful minced parsley.
Boiled dressing.
¼ teaspoonful pepper.
Hard boiled eggs.

For the dressing use the following

Materials:

1 cup vinegar.
2 teaspoonfuls sugar.
1 teaspoonful mustard.
5 tablespoonfuls butter.
1 teaspoonful salt.
¼ teaspoonful pepper.
1 cup sweet milk.
2 eggs.

Way of Preparing Dressing and Salad:

Melt the butter, add the salt, sugar, mustard and pepper, then add the vinegar and bring to a boil. Then stir in the milk. Stir constantly until thick. Remove from the fire and fold in the two well-beaten eggs. When ready to serve, line the salad bowl with lettuce, put in a layer of the potatoes and sprinkle with the chopped onion, celery and parsley. Alternate in this manner until all the materials are used with a layer of dressing on top.

Garnish with hard-boiled eggs in quarters, and the white leaves of the celery.

The plain French dressing may be used with the salad.

SANDWICHES

Sandwiches as a distinct dish, are specifically English and American.

They are used particularly for cold repasts, cold lunches and especially for outdoor refreshments at summer picnics and excursions.

Sandwiches are easily made and require for their perfection only daintiness.

Their variety is great, and largely depends upon the ingenuity of the maker.

Chicken Salad Sandwiches.

Between two thin, oblong slices of bread, buttered, place a layer of chicken salad on a lettuce leaf.

In making chicken salad for sandwiches, chop the chicken and celery much finer than for ordinary purposes.

Fig Sandwich.

Thin slices of bread, cut in fancy shapes, and buttered, with fig-filling between each two.

The fig-filling should be prepared as follows:

One-half a pound finely chopped figs, one-third cup of sugar, half a cup of boiling water, and two tablespoonfuls of lemon juice. Mix these ingredients and cook in a double boiler until thick enough to spread.

Lettuce Sandwiches.

Thin, oblong slices of buttered bread, with a filling of lettuce leaves, dipped in mayonnaise and sprinkled with parmesan cheese.

Nut-Ginger Sandwiches.

Take three long, thin slices of bread, buttered. Between the first and second place a layer of chopped, preserved ginger, mixed with cream and between the second and third slices place a layer of chopped English walnuts, then tie up each sandwich neatly with baby ribbon.

Nut Sandwiches.

Thin slices of whole-wheat bread, cut circular, and buttered. The filling should be made of chopped, roasted and salted peanuts, mixed with sufficient mayonnaise to spread easily.

Ribbon Sandwiches.

Take three square, thin slices of white bread and two corresponding slices of whole-wheat. Butter them and place between each two slices, the white bread being on the outside, a filling made of egg-paste. Take a sharp knife and cut crosswise into thin slices, each five (three white, two whole-wheat) slices of bread cut into six sandwiches.

Egg-paste is prepared by mashing the yolks of three hard boiled eggs to a paste and adding two tablespoonfuls of salad dressing and pepper and salt to taste.

SAUCES & PRESERVES

"Hunger is the best sauce."

Elaborate French sauces are of exquisite flavor but mysterious and difficult to make, and they are rarely attempted in the average household.

With the following simple recipes, however, with good materials and careful, unhurried attention, all will succeed.

These delicate, velvety sauces will go far toward making any meal enjoyable.

BROWN SAUCE.

Materials:

1 heaping tablespoonful butter.

1 tablespoonful chopped onion.

1 tablespoonful chopped carrot.

1 tablespoonful chopped parsley.

1 tablespoonful flour.

1 cup boiling water.

1 teaspoonful beef extract.

1 tablespoonful tomato catsup.

1 teaspoonful caramel coloring.

Way of Preparing:

Melt your butter in a frying pan, add the chopped vegetables and cook ten minutes, taking care not to burn the butter. Then add the flour and stir until it is a light brown. Gradually add the boiling water, beef extract, salt, tomato catsup and lastly the coloring. Cook five minutes and strain. It is then ready for use.

Two tablespoonfuls of chopped mushrooms can be added if

Mushroom Sauce

is wanted.

CARAMEL COLORING.

Materials:

1 pint sugar. 1 pint cold water.

Way of Preparing:

Melt the sugar in a saucepan over a brisk fire.
Cook until it is a dark brown, and almost burned.
It will be hard and brittle and bitter to the taste.
Now add slowly the cold water, stirring all the
time. Boil until it is as thick as molasses. If too
thick add water and boil again. Put in bottles.
Keep corked and it will never spoil.

This is used for coloring soups, sauces, gravies
and in cake making.

HORSE RADISH SAUCE.

Materials:

1 cup cream, scalded. ½ teaspoonful salt.
2 tablespoonfuls freshly
grated horseradish.

Way of Preparing:

Place the cream in a double boiler and bring
to the boiling point, add the horse radish, cook two
minutes and remove from the fire, then add the
salt and serve.

LEMON SAUCE.

Materials:

1 cup sugar. 1 heaping tablespoonful.
1 tablespoonful flour. butter.
Pinch salt. 1½ cups boiling water.
½ lemon, sliced.

Way of Preparing:

Mix the sugar and flour, add the boiling water,
put on the fire and when it begins to boil add the
butter, sliced lemon and salt. Cook until it has the
consistency of cream. Remove from the fire and
serve either hot or cold.

Orange Sauce

is made by substituting one orange for the lemon,
and

Chocolate Sauce

by adding two squares of Baker's unsweetened
chocolate to the orange sauce.

MINT SAUCE.

Materials:

2 doz. (one bunch) 2 tablespoonfuls sugar.
sprigs of mint. Juice of one lemon.
½ cup of boiling water. ½ teaspoonful salt.

Way of Preparing:

Chop the mint leaves very fine, and pour over
them the boiling water, let stand for half an hour,
then add the lemon juice, the salt and sugar.

TARTARE SAUCE.

is one cup of mayonnaise with the addition of one tablespoonful of chopped capers, olives or pickles, and one teaspoonful of onion juice.

TOMATO SAUCE.

Materials:

1 can tomatoes.	2 tablespoonfuls butter.
1 stalk celery.	2 tablespoonfuls flour.
1 small onion, sliced.	1 teaspoonful beef ex-
2 sprigs parsley.	tract.
1 bay leaf.	Salt and pepper.

Way of Preparing:

Cook the tomatoes, celery, onion, parsley and bay leaf twenty-five minutes, strain and return to the double boiler. Cream butter and flour together, and add them to the previous mixture, then add the beef extract and salt and pepper to taste. It is then ready to serve.

If thicker than desired, thin with boiling water.

WHITE SAUCE.

Materials:

1 cup of milk.	2 tablespoonfuls butter.
1 tablespoonful flour.	½ teaspoonful salt.
¼ teaspoonful white pepper.	½ teaspoonful onion juice.

Way of Preparing:

Heat the milk in a double boiler, cream butter and flour together and add them to the milk. Cook until it has the consistency of cream; add the salt, pepper and onion juice, cook one minute longer and serve.

Note.—When using this sauce for sweetbreads or chicken, substitute one tablespoonful of orange juice for the onion juice. When using it for oysters, substitute two tablespoonfuls of sherry wine for the onion juice and add half a cup of thick sweet cream.

FRUIT SAUCES AND PRESERVES.

CLARIFIED APPLES.

Materials:

1 cup water.	6 large tart apples.
2 cups sugar.	½ lemon.

Way of Preparing:

Make a syrup of the sugar and water. Peel the apples, cut each in six pieces and cook in the hot syrup until clear. Remove from the syrup and place in a glass dish. When all the apples are cooked add the lemon rind and juice to the syrup. Boil it until thick, remove the lemon rind and pour over the apples.

In peeling the apples, peel and cook but two at a time if you wish them to be a very light yellow in color. If the apples are crowded in the kettle you cannot handle them easily, and if allowed to stand after peeling, they will turn dark.

Quantity:

This will serve six.

CRANBERRY SAUCE.

In making cranberry sauce do not use any water in the cooking. Wash and pick the berries and put them in a double boiler to cook. Stir them when they begin to soften, and when they are reduced to an even pulp remove them from the fire and pass them through a colander. Return to the fire and sweeten to taste.

Cook long enough to melt and combine the sugar. This makes a stiff jelly. If you wish it thinner add a little water when cooking the second time.

RHUBARB SAUCE.

Should be made in the same manner as cranberry sauce.

GINGER PEARS.

Materials:

1 quart preserved ginger.	8 lbs. pears.
	6 lbs. sugar.
Juice of five lemons.	2 oranges.
Rind of five lemons.	Hot water.

Way of Preparing:

Cut the ginger in thin slices. Press out the juice of the five lemons and the oranges and cut their rind into shreds. Peel the pears and cut them crosswise in the slices. Add enough hot water to the sugar to dissolve the latter. When hot add the lemon juice, orange juice, ginger, lemon rind and orange peel. Lastly add the pears and cook slowly three hours. Place in pint fruit jars and seal. Keep in cool dry place.

TOO MANY COOKS
SPOIL THE BROTH

Of a good beginning cometh a good end.
—John Heywoode (1565).

Soups are of two classes: soups made with "stock" and soups without.

To the former class belong bouillon, brown stock, white stock, consommé and lambstock or mutton-broth.

Soups without stock are classed as cream soups, purèes and bisques.

Soups often take their names from the different nations using them.

BOUILLON.

Materials:

3 lbs lean beef.	1-3 cup potatoes,
2 lbs lean veal.	1-3 cup celery,
1 lb. marrowbone.	1-3 cup onion,
6 cups cold water.	1-3 cup turnip,
10 pepper corns.	finely chopped.
1 tablespoonful salt.	

Way of Preparing:

Put the meat and marrow bone into the soup kettle. Put in the water and let it stand covered one hour. Heat slowly to the boiling point. Remove the scum and cook for four hours. Add the vegetables and seasoning and cook two hours. Strain and allow it to get cold. Remove the fat when it is cold. Serve in cups.

Quantity:

This will serve six people.

ICED BOUILLON.

This is plain bouillon with the addition of Madeira wine or sherry, according to taste. Have it very cold when serving.

BROWN STOCK.

Materials:

5 lbs. shin beef.	1-3 cup potato,
½ gallon water.	1-3 cup turnip,
10 pepper corns.	1-3 cup onion,
5 cloves.	1-3 cup carrot,
1 bay leaf.	1-3 cup celery,
1 tablespoonful salt.	coarsely chopped.
2 sprigs parsley.	

Way of Preparing:

Cut the lean meat in inch pieces and brown it in a hot frying pan, using the marrow from the bone. Put the bone and fat in the kettle. Add the cold water and let it stand for twenty minutes. Put it over the fire and bring it to the boiling point. Remove the scum as it rises and add the browned meat. Cover the kettle. Reduce heat and cook the meat at the boiling point for five hours. Add the prepared vegetables and seasoning and cook for two hours.

Strain and cool immediately.

Quantity:

This will serve six persons.

CREAM OF CELERY SOUP.

Materials:

2 cups white stock.	3 tablespoonfuls flour.
2 cups celery (cut in inch pieces).	1 pint milk.
	½ pint cream.
2 cups hot water.	1 teaspoonful salt.
1 small onion.	½ teaspoonful white
3 tablespoonfuls butter.	pepper.

Way of Preparing:

Parboil celery in water for fifteen minutes, drain and add the celery to the stock. Cook until the celery is very soft. Rub it through a sieve. Scald the onion in the milk. Remove the onion and add the milk to the stock. Cream the flour and butter together and add them also to the stock. Lastly add the cream and season with the salt and pepper.

Quantity:

The above will serve six persons.

Note.—Other cream soups are made in the same manner by using the particular vegetable instead of celery.

CREAM OF TOMATO SOUP.

Materials:

½ can tomatoes.
1 quart sweet milk.
1 tablespoonful sugar.
1 small onion.
1 pinch of soda.
2 tablespoonfuls flour.
3 tablespoonfuls butter.
1 teaspoonful salt.
¼ teaspoonful pepper.
½ cup cold water.

Way of Preparing:

Scald the milk with the onion. Remove the onion and add the flour mixed with the water, taking care to keep the mixture free from lumps. Cook the tomatoes fifteen minutes. Add the sugar and soda and pass through a sieve. Combine the mixtures and add the butter and seasoning.

Strain into a tureen and serve at once.

Quantity:

The above soup will serve six persons.

GUMBO.

Materials:

1 large chicken, jointed
1 tomato, sliced.
1 onion, sliced.
2 dozen okras.
1 red pepper minced.
1 slice ham, cut in small pieces.
1 pint shrimps, shelled.
1 tablespoonful lard.
1 teaspoonful flour.
Rice.
Salt to taste.
2 quarts water.

Way of Preparing:

Put the lard into a hot soup kettle. Fry the onion a light brown in the lard. Then add the flour, the tomato, ham, chicken and okras. Fry all ten minutes, add the water and cook slowly for one and one-half hours. Remove the chicken, cut it into small pieces and return it to the kettle. Add the shrimps and cook twenty minutes.

Serve with plain boiled rice cooked very dry.

Quantity:

This will serve six persons.

MULLIGATAWNY SOUP.

Materials:

5 cups white stock.
1 pint raw chicken.
   (cut in dice).
1 cup tomatoes.
½ cup of onion.
½ cup of celery.
½ cup carrot.
1 pepper, chopped.
2 tablespoonfuls butter.
3 tablespoonfuls flour.
2 sprigs parsley.
3 cloves.
1 blade mace.
1 apple, sliced.
1 teaspoonful curry powder.
Salt and pepper.

Way of Preparing:

Cook the vegetables and chicken in butter until brown. Add the flour, mace, curry powder, cloves, parsley, tomatoes and stock and simmer one hour. Strain, reserving the chicken and rub the vegetables through a sieve, add the chicken to the soup, season with salt and pepper (according to taste) and serve with boiled rice.

The apple is included in the vegetables.

Quantity:

This will serve eight persons.

OXTAIL SOUP.

Materials:

1 oxtail cut in small pieces.	1 teaspoonful salt.
	¼ teaspoonful pepper.
5 cups brown stock.	½ cup Madeira wine.
Carrot cut in dice.	1 teaspoonful Worces-
Celery cut in dice.	tershire sauce.
Onion cut in dice.	Juice of half lemon.
Turnip cut in dice.	Butter.

Way of Preparing:

Dredge the oxtail in flour and fry in butter until nicely browned. Add it to the stock and simmer two hours. Parboil the vegetables ten minutes, drain them and add them to the stock. Cook until the vegetables are tender, then add salt, pepper, wine, sauce and lemon juice. Let it cook ten minutes and serve.

Quantity:

This will serve six persons.

POTATO SOUP.

Materials:

3 potatoes.	1 teaspoonful salt.
1 quart milk.	¼ teaspoonful pepper.
1 onion.	2 tablespoonfuls butter.
2 stalks celery.	1 tablespoonful flour.

Way of Preparing:

Cook the potatoes in salted water with the onion. When soft mash the potatoes smooth and rub through a fine sieve. Scald the milk with the celery. Remove the celery and add the butter and flour creamed together. Then add the prepared potatoes to the milk and season with the salt and pepper. Let it come to a boil and serve at once.

Quantity:

This soup will serve six persons.

SPLIT PEA SOUP.

Materials:

1 cup dried split peas.	1 teaspoonful salt.
2 quarts cold water.	¼ teaspoonful white
1 pint milk.	pepper.
1 small onion.	2-inch cube salt pork.
2 tablespoonfuls butter.	2 tablespoonfuls flour.

Way of Preparing:

Soak the peas over night, drain and add the water, pork and onion, sliced. Simmer until the peas are very soft, and then rub them through a sieve. Cream the butter and flour together and add to the peas. Then add salt, pepper and milk. Reheat and serve hot.

Quantity:

This will serve six persons.

WHITE STOCK.

Materials:

4 lbs. knuckle of veal.	1 small onion.
1 lb. lean beef.	2 stalks celery.
2½ quarts cold water.	1 bayleaf.
10 pepper corns.	1 tablespoonful salt.

Way of Preparing:

Remove the meat from the bone and cut it in small pieces. Do the same with the beef, only make the pieces smaller. Put meat and bone into a kettle and add the water. Bring it slowly to a boil and skim carefully. Simmer for five hours. Strain twice through several thicknesses of cheesecloth and the stock will be clear. White stock can be made from the water in which a fowl or chicken is cooked.

Quantity:

The above recipe will produce three pints of soup-stock.

VEGETABLES

Vegetables should first of all be fresh, or at least perfectly preserved.

In planning meals, consider the appropriate place for certain vegetables with different meats. Vegetables and the mode of preparing them should be varied from day to day, but any fresh, green vegetable served very cold, or any well-cooked vegetable served very hot will always be appreciated.

Boiled vegetables should be cooked in an abundance of salted water, and served quickly, as soon as they are done.

It is considered a valuable secret by some French cooks, that green vegetables will retain their bright color if boiled in an open kettle.

AUSTRIAN CARROTS.

Materials:

1 quart of carrots.	½ cup vinegar.
1 quart water.	¾ cup sugar.
1 teaspoonful salt.	1 tablespoonful butter.

Way of Preparing:

Scrape the carrots and cut them in sections one and one-half inches long, then slice them lengthwise one-fourth of an inch thick and then in strips of the same thickness. Add the water and salt and boil them until tender. Drain off the water, add the vinegar, sugar and butter, and cook until the carrots have a clear, transparent appearance. Then serve.

Quantity:

This will serve five persons.

CARAMELIZED SWEET POTATOES.

Materials:

1 dozen small sweet potatoes.
1 pint brown sugar.
1 cup hot water.
2 quarts hot water.
1 tablespoonful butter.
1 teaspoonful salt.
½ teaspoonful cinnamon.

Way of Preparing:

Boil the potatoes in two quarts of hot water until they are tender. Peel and arrange in a shallow baking dish. Boil the cup of water and sugar together for ten minutes. Sprinkle salt and cinnamon over the potatoes and add the butter to the sauce. Then pour the sauce over the potatoes and bake in a moderate oven until the potatoes are nicely browned.

Serve in the dish in which they were baked.

Quantity:

This will serve six people.

DEVILED POTATOES.

Materials:

2 dozen small new potatoes.
1 teaspoonful salt.
2 tablespoonfuls vinegar.
1 teaspoonful mustard.
2 heaping tablespoonfuls butter.
1 cup lard.
2 egg yolks.
¼ teaspoonful pepper.

Way of Preparing:

Boil the potatoes until nearly done. Peel them, heat the lard in a frying pan and fry the potatoes until they are a nice golden-brown color. Melt the butter in a saucepan and add the pepper, salt, mustard and vinegar. Now place the potatoes in the saucepan and let them simmer three minutes. Remove to a hot dish. Add the eggs to the sauce. Pour it over the potatoes and serve.

Quantity:

Two dozen potatoes to serve six.

EGG PLANT.

Materials:

1 large egg plant.
2 eggs.
1 quart boiling water.
½ cup flour.
1 tablespoonful salt.
Deep fat.
1 cup cracker crumbs.

Way of Preparing:

Cut your egg plant into one-half inch slices.
Remove the peel. Pour over it the quart of boiling
water after dissolving it in the salt. Let it stand
one hour, drain off the water, wipe the slices dry,
flour lightly, dip in beaten egg, and then in the
crumbs and fry in the deep fat. Serve very hot.

Quantity:

This will serve five persons.

GREEN PEPPERS STUFFED WITH CORN.

Materials:

6 large sweet peppers.	½ cup cream.
2 cups green corn.	½ cup boiling water.
3 tablespoonfuls butter.	1 teaspoonful salt.
3 tablespoonfuls boil-ing water.	½ teaspoonful pepper.

Way of Preparing:

With a sharp knife cut around three-fourths of
the stem end of each pepper, leaving it hinged by
the other fourth as a lid. Remove the seeds and
inner membranes. Cover the pepper with cold
water, and bring it to a boil. Drain off the water,
cover them with fresh boiling water and simmer
until tender. Drain, sprinkle lightly with salt, and
allow to cool. Put two tablespoonfuls of butter into
a frying pan and heat it. When hot add the green
corn and the three tablespoonfuls of hot water.
Cook five minutes and add the cream and seasonings. Now cook slowly until quite thick. Let the
mixture then cool and fill your prepared peppers
with it. Fasten down the stem-end lids of the peppers and place them in a buttered baking dish.
Melt the remaining tablespoonful of butter in the
half cup of boiling water, pour the liquid over the
peppers and bake for twenty-five minutes. These
will be found delicious to serve with fish courses.

Quantity:

This will serve six people.

HASHED BROWN POTATOES WITH GRAVY.

Materials:

3 cups cold, boiled po-tatoes, sliced.	1 teaspoonful salt.
1 onion.	½ teaspoonful pepper.
1 tablespoonful flour.	½ bayleaf.
1 cup boiling water.	1 tablespoonful tomato catsup.
3 tablespoonfuls butter.	

Way of Preparing:

Melt one tablespoonful of butter in a saucepan, add the flour and brown carefully; then add a cup of boiling water, leaving out three tablespoonfuls of it. Now add the salt, pepper, one-half the onion (sliced thin), and the half bay leaf. Melt one tablespoonful of butter in the three of boiling water and moisten your potatoes with this mixture. Rub a frying pan with the other half of the onion, place in it a tablespoonful of butter and heat very hot. Pour in the prepared potatoes and brown. Turn the potatoes out like an omelette onto a hot platter, strain the gravy and add the tomato catsup. Serve the strained gravy in a sauceboat with the potatoes, or pour it around them on the platter.

Quantity:

This will serve six persons.

RICE.

Wash and cleanse the rice. Then pour boiling hot water on it—half a gallon of water to one cup of raw rice—and let it boil without stirring it for from twenty-five to thirty minutes, according to the quality of your rice. When the kernels, although each seems separate and independent, are soft, pour off the water, return it to the fire and let it steam until it seems dry. Then your rice is done and you may serve it either with brown butter, or with sugar and cream, or with sugar and powdered cinnamon mixed, or with the juice or gravy of any roast.

SCALLOPED CABBAGE.

Materials:

1 quart cabbage, prepared as for slaw.	1 tablespoonful flour.
1 teaspoonful salt.	1 teaspoonful salt.
1 quart boiling water.	½ teaspoonful pepper.
1 cup sweet milk.	1 cup fine cracker crumbs.
2 tablespoonfuls butter.	1 tablespoonful butter.

Way of Preparing:

Pour the boiling water on the cabbage and add one teaspoonful of salt. Boil fifteen minutes. Drain off the water. Heat the milk, cream the two tablespoonfuls of butter and the flour and add them to the milk. Then add one teaspoonful of salt and the pepper. Cook to the consistency of thick cream. Remove from the fire. Butter a small pudding dish and sprinkle the bottom with cracker crumbs. Put in half your cabbage, then half the sauce, sprinkle with cracker crumbs, then add the remaining cabbage, then the sauce and cover thickly

with cracker crumbs. Dot it with small pieces of
butter, cover and bake in a moderate oven twenty-
five minutes, uncover and brown. **Serve from the**
dish in which it was baked.

Quantity:

This will serve six persons.

STUFFED ONIONS.

Materials:

6 large onions.
1 cup finely chopped
    raw beef.
1 cup soft bread
    crumbs.
1 teaspoonful salt.
½ teaspoonful pepper.

1 egg.
¼ cup cream.
1 tablespoonful melted
    butter.
½ cup cracker crumbs.
1 tablespoonful boiling
    water.

Way of Preparing:

Peel and parboil the onions in salted water ten
minutes, remove and drain. When cooled remove
the center of each onion. Add the cream and well-
beaten egg to the boiling water. To this add the
bread crumbs and the chopped beef, together with
the seasonings and fill the centers of the onions
with this mixture. Brush the top of the onions
with melted butter, sprinkle with cracker crumbs,
place in a shallow, buttered baking dish, cover it
and bake until onions are tender, then uncover **and**
continue baking until they are brown.

Quantity:

This will serve six persons.

STUFFED TOMATOES.

Materials:

8 medium-sized firm
    tomatoes.
1 cup cold chicken,
    chopped fine.
1 tablespoonful salt.
1 cup cracker crumbs.

1 teaspoonful onion
    juice.
1 cup of soup stock.
1 egg.
2 tablespoonfuls cream.
1 pinch pepper.
Toast.

Way of Preparing:

Cut a small slice from the top of each tomato,
and scoop out the pulp with a spoon. Sprinkle the
tomatoes on the inside with salt. Turn them up-
side down on a platter and let them stand half an
hour. Remove the seeds from the pulps, drain off
the juice and make a stuffing, using the chopped
chicken, tomato pulp, cracker crumbs, egg, cream,
onion juice, pepper and a teaspoonful of salt.
Wipe the tomatoes dry inside and out and fill each
with the prepared stuffing. Place in a baking dish,
pour the soup stock around them and bake in a
moderately hot oven until the tomatoes are tender,
but not falling to pieces. You should baste the to-

matoes frequently with the stock while baking. Serve immediately, placing each tomato on a square of toast.

Quantity:

This will serve eight people.

TENNESSEE CORN.

Materials:

1 quart green corn.	2 tablespoonfuls melted butter.
2 eggs.	
1 teaspoonful salt.	3 tablespoonfuls cream.
½ teaspoonful pepper.	1 cup milk.

Way of Preparing:

With a sharp knife cut enough green corn from the cobs to fill a quart measure. Heat the milk. Beat the eggs and add to them the cream and seasonings, then add the butter, and scalded milk. Place the corn in a buttered pudding dish, and pour the liquid mixture over it. Bake in a slow oven until firm. Serve hot as a side dish with a meat course.

Quantity:

This will serve six persons.

HINTS *for* HOUSEKEEPERS

China Cement.

Take dissolved gum arabic and stir in enough plaster of Paris to make a soft paste. This is almost colorless and acts excellently as cement for China. Very delicate china or porcelain has the pieces tied carefully in place with tape. It is then put into a saucepan of milk and the latter is very gradually brought to the boiling point. Remove the saucepan from the fire, but leave the china in it for about six minutes. Lift out carefully and place on a shelf to dry.

Rust Stains on White Goods.

Lemon juice and salt will remove rust stains from linen or muslin without affecting the white goods. Let the sun shine on the goods after having moistened the spots with the mixture—two or three applications may be necessary.

Grass Stains on Clothing.

Should be saturated with alcohol for a little time, then wash in clear water.

Kerosene Oil.

Coal oil will help the housekeeper out of many difficulties.

A spoonful of Kerosene added to a kettle of very hot water will make windows, looking-glasses and picture glasses bright and clear. Use a small, clean cloth, wring it dry and rub it over the glass, after wiping down the framework with an oiled cloth. Then proceed to the next window and treat it similarly on both sides. After that go back to the first one and wipe it dry with a large clean cloth.

No real polishing is required, and the window or glass will look clear and shiny.

Kerosene will clean your hands better than anything else after blacking a range or stove. Pour a little in the water, wash your hands in it, then wash them in tepid water, and finally with plenty of soap, and a stiff nail brush in hot water. Finish up by rubbing the hands with lemon and rosewater and glycerine.

When your kitchen sink is rusty, rub it over with kerosene.

Squeaky shoes are cured by dipping the soles in kerosene. Enough to reach the top of the soles without reaching the upper leather.

The white spots appearing in the spring on the lining of your refrigerator will disappear if you rub the zinc with kerosene. Leave the refrigerator open several hours, then wash with water, soap and some ammonia. The refrigerator will then be clean and sweet and all spots will have disappeared.

To Soften Boots and Shoes.

Rub your shoes and boots well with castor oil and let them stand twelve hours. This will keep them from cracking and make them yielding and soft.

Ink Spots On Fingers.

Ink is removed from the fingers in a very simple manner. Wet the finger and then rub the phosphorus end of a match on the spot. Wipe the fingers and renew the action until the spot has disappeared in a minute or two.

Keeping Olive Oil Sweet.

Always keep olive oil in the refrigerator tightly corked. Never put more than two days' supply into your table cruet.

Cooling Beds in Summertime.

A piece of Chinese Matting slipped between the sheet and the mattress will be found to be decidedly cooling. A hot water bag, filled with ice-water laid under the pillow will have the same effect.

Molasses.

If molasses tastes acid, put a teaspoon of soda in each cupful of molasses.

Cleaning Paint.

Put two ounces of soda in a quart of hot water, and wash with it, rinsing the paint off with pure water.

Curing Hangnails.

A small quantity of Collodion procured at any drug store, applied with a small brush to the skin around the nails will have the desired effect in from three to four days in curing hangnails.

Collodion is excellent in cases of burns or cuts. It excludes air and dust.

Cure for Toothache.

Heat two tablespoonfuls of vinegar. Dip a little absorbent cotton in the hot vinegar and apply it to the gum at the root of the aching tooth.

Releasing Ice Cream or Jelly from Molds.

Fold a hot cloth around the mold and jelly or ices will leave the mold without sticking.

Removing Starch from Irons.

Should starch cling to your iron while using it, sprinkle some salt on a piece of brown paper and run the iron on it.

MENUS

"This folio of four pages, happy work,
Which not e'en critics criticise."

In household cooking, consult the tastes of the family, and adapt the menus of the different days to include the favorite dishes of each member. With or without guests, a charming hostess may observe a plain and easy style of entertaining.

The smaller the dinner, the more surety of its being well-planned and served, and thoroughly successful.

The housekeeper needs not so much technical knowledge as everyday appreciation of what is good and healthful to eat.

A poor table may be wasteful.

To dine with comfort and pleasure, to promote health, and at the same time to keep the cook good-natured and happy, the diner and the dinner should be ready at the same time.

The hot dishes should be hot and the cold dishes always cold. To have your coffee and salad both lukewarm is ruinous indeed.

Menu of the Breakfast in Honor of Prince Henry of Prussia, given by the Germania Club at Chicago, March 4th, 1902.

Grape Fruit,
Clam Broth, "Uncle Sam,"
Celery,   Olives,   Radishes,
Planked Lake Superior Whitefish,
(1897 Oberemmler. Elserberg.)
Potatoes Jeannette,
Fresh Mushrooms on Toast,
Broiled Breast of Spring Chicken,
(Pol Roger, Cuvee de Reserve, 1889.)
Hearts of Lettuce Salad,
Camembert Cheese,
Salt Crusts.
Coffee.
(Apollinaris.)

CHRISTMAS DINNER.

Consomme in Cups.

Fish Premier with Premier Sauce.

Potato Balls.　　　　　　　　　　Cold Slaw.

Roasted Young Goose.

Horseradish.　　　　　　　　Apple Sauce.

Pineapple Fritters with Wine Sauce.

Orange and Grape Salad.

Plum Pudding, Brandy Sauce.　　　Mince Pie.

New York Ice Cream.

Raisins.　　　　　　　　　　Nuts.

Black Coffee.

Decorations.—Christmas wreaths, Holly, Mistletoe, Table lighted with Red Candles in silver candlesticks.

EASTER DINNER.

Cream of Spinach Soup.

Fried Trout with Tartar Sauce.

Nut Bread Sandwiches,

Potato Croquettes,　　　　　Green Peas,

Crown of Lamb with Mint Sauce,

Banana Fritters with Orange Sauce,

Sweetbreads, Gomez Style,

Lettuce and Tomato Salad,

Pineapple and Orange Sherbet,

Assorted Cakes,

Candied Mintleaves,　　Candied Orange Peels,

Black Coffee.

Decorations.—Daffodils and white tulips.

NEW YEAR'S TEA.

Creamed Oysters in Chafing Dish,

Celery and Nut Salad,

Cold Turkey with Cranberry Jelly,

Creamed Potatoes,

Almond Tarts,

Maple Perfect with White Fruit Cake,

Bonbons,　　　　　　　　Salted Peanuts,

Chocolate,　　　　Tea.

Decorations.—American Beauty Roses in the center. An individual flower at each plate.

PINK AND GREEN LUNCH.

Oyster Cocktail Sprinkled with Chopped Parsley.

Cream of Spinach Soup,

Salmon Croquettes with Green Peas,

Lettuce and Tomato Salad,

Hot Shamrock Rolls,

Pistachio and Strawberry Ice Creams,

Creme de Menthe.

Decorations.—Pink Sweet Peas and Mignonette.

THANKSGIVING DINNER.

Cream of Celery Soup,
Scalloped Oysters,
Celery,   Olives,
Roast Turkey,
Garnished with Sausage Cakes,
Mashed Potatoes, Clarified Sweet Potatoes,
Sweet Pickles,
Cranberry Sherbet,
Asparagus Salad,
Caramel Ice Cream,   Hot Apple Pie,
Neufchatel Cheese,
Crackers,   Coffee.

Decorations.—Centerpiece; fruits in basket made
of Pumpkin surrounded with autumn leaves, chrys-
anthemums and grasses.
The fruits can be served last if desired.

WEDDING BREAKFAST.

Natural Strawberries,
Broiled Halibut with Hothouse Cucumbers,
Peas in White Sauce,
Hot Rolls,
Broiled Chicken Breasts with
Mushroom Sauce,
Lettuce Heart and White Asparagus Salad,
Fruit Ices,
Assorted Cakes,
Bonbons,   Salted Nuts,
Coffee.

Decorations.—Brides' Roses and Maidenhair
Ferns.

Note.—Add a Bride's Cake, if desired.

Table of Weights and Measures.

3 teaspoonfuls of a liquid equal 1 tablespoonful.

4 tablespoonfuls of a liquid equal ½ gill or ¼ cup.

½ cup equals 1 gill.

2 gills equal 1 cup.

2 cups equal 1 pint.

2 pints (4 cups) equal 1 quart.

4 cups of flour equal 1 pound or 1 quart.

2 cups of butter, solid, equal 1 pound.

½ cup of butter, solid, equals ¼ pound, 4 ounces.

2 cups of granulated sugar equal 1 pound.

2½ cups of powdered sugar equal 1 pound.

1 pint of milk or water equals 1 pound.

1 pint chopped meat equals 1 pound.

10 eggs, shelled equal 1 pound.

8 eggs with shells equal 1 pound.

2 tablespoonfuls of butter equal 1 ounce.

2 tablespoonfuls of granulated sugar 1 ounce.

4 tablespoonfuls of flour equal 1 ounce.

4 tablespoonfuls of coffee equal 1 ounce.

1 tablespoonful of liquid equals ½ ounce.

4 tablespoonfuls of butter equal 2 ounces or ¼ cup.

All measurements are level unless otherwise stated in the recipe.

INDEX

NOTES

·NOTES·

NOTES

the Wind Wagon

by Celia Barker Lottridge

Illustrated by Daniel Clifford

Silver Burdett Press
Parsippany, New Jersey

For my father C.B.L.

*To my wife Loretta and
my children Anna and James* D.C.

Text © 1995 by Celia Barker Lottridge
Illustrations © 1995 by Daniel Clifford

Published by Silver Burdett Press
A Simon and Schuster Company
299 Jefferson Road, Parsippany, NJ 07054

Designed by Sue Kyong Suk Brooks

Printed in the United States of America
10 9 8 7 6 5 4 3 2 1

Library of Congress Cataloging-in-Publication Data
Lottridge, Celia Barker.
The Wind Wagon/by Celia Barker Lottridge:
illustrated by Daniel Clifford. p. cm.
Summary: Sam Peppard, a blacksmith in 1860's Kansas,
builds a prairie schooner that sails to Denver, Colorado,
powered by wind.
1. Peppard, Sam—Juvenile fiction. [1. Peppard, Sam—
Fiction. 2. Wagons—Fiction. 3. Frontier and pioneer
life—Fiction. 4. Prairies—Fiction.] I. Clifford, Daniel,
ill. II. Title.

PZ7.L918Wi 1995 94-399398
[Fic]--dc20 CIP AC

ISBN 0-382-24927-5 (LSB) ISBN 0-382-24928-3 (JHC)
ISBN 0-382-24929-1 (SC)

Chapter 1

SAM PEPPARD ARRIVED in the town of Oskaloosa on a summer day in 1859. The folks gossiping in front of the general store watched him jump down from the freight wagon that was making its regular stop with passengers and goods.

"There's another young fellow looking for a new life in Kansas Territory," said Joe Willard. Everybody laughed since Joe was a young fellow himself who had arrived not more than six months before.

3

Sam wasn't noticing the town folk, though. He was noticing the wind. It was a strong wind from the southwest, and it flattened Sam's denim shirt against his back and tried to lift his broad-brimmed hat off his head. Sam took a deep breath of the sweet smell of prairie grass and dust warmed by the sun.

"That's the smell of the West," said Joe. "Some folks get one whiff and travel on."

"Not me," said Sam. "I want to settle here." But there was a bit of regret in his eye as he watched the freight wagon rattle away. Then he got a grip on his hat and took a look at Oskaloosa.

He saw a few flat-fronted wooden buildings around a square that might, someday, have a courthouse in its center. The sidewalks were wooden, too, and the streets were dirt. Oskaloosa was a brand-new town just getting started in the rolling hills on the edge of the western plains.

"I reckon that this town needs a black-smith," Sam said to Joe. He pointed to his bundle of tools. "That's good for me because I'm a blacksmith. I like this place. It's right on the edge of the east and the west and the north and the south. Someday it will be dead center of this country—just where I want to be."

So Sam opened up a smithy on the north side of the square, next to the livery stable. He was right. Oskaloosa did need a black-smith to make wagon-wheel rims and nails and hinges and to shoe horses and mules. Besides, folks needed a place to hang around and talk, and Sam's shop suited them just fine. They would stand around the forge and tell the latest news or listen to Sam's stories about his travels.

Sam lived in a room behind his shop. Every morning before he opened up he would step out the front door and test the wind. If it blew from the north, south, or west, he

would step right back in and start to work. But if the wind was from the east, he would stand facing west in the middle of the street and stretch his arms out while the wind whipped his shirttails around his ears.

Folks got used to the sight, but they teased Sam about it. Some said, "You be careful, Sam. That wind is gonna blow you straight to Denver someday."

"I'd rather go by wind than by oxcart," Sam would say.

The country around Oskaloosa was a jumping-off place for people traveling west. Just north ran the Oregon Trail and just south ran the Santa Fe Trail. But whatever trail people took, they all went by oxcart. Prairie schooners, they were called, and they lumbered over the flat prairie at a mighty slow rate.

Sam thought about all those miles of waving prairie grass. "If that was water, with real schooners sailing before the wind, it would be a pretty sight," he said to Joe.

"It's a beautiful thought," said Joe, grinning, "only there isn't any water."

"There's plenty of wind, though," said Sam and he began to make a plan.

One winter day the folks who made a habit of warming themselves beside Sam's smithy fire found him building something. It looked like a wagon box. Funny shape, though, kind of narrow.

"Eight feet long, three feet wide," Sam said when they asked him about it, but he wouldn't explain why he was building it.

He wouldn't explain why the wheels were so high either or why the metal rims were so thick. When they asked him why he was fiddling around with some contraption at the rear of the wagon and where the horse or the ox was going to be hitched, Sam just said, "This isn't a horsecart or an oxcart. You'll see."

One morning, Joe went into Sam's shop and found Sam fixing something that looked very much like a mast in the front of the wagon. "Exactly what *is* this thing you're building?" he said. "Are you aiming to put a sail to a wagon?"

"Joe," said Sam, "I'm aiming to use the wind. There's more wind than anything else out there on the prairie. It blows east. It blows west. It blows north and south. Why can't it take folks along with it? Think of it, Joe—sails across the prairie."

Joe shook his head, but he caught a little of what Sam was seeing. "You gonna call it a sailing wagon?"

"A wind wagon. That's what it is—a wind wagon," said Sam Peppard.

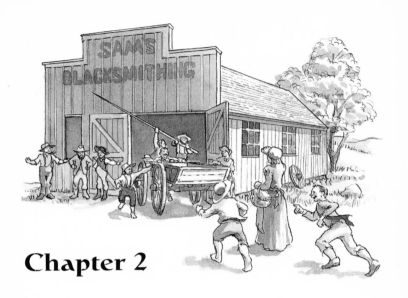

Chapter 2

BY TEN O'CLOCK that morning, news of Sam's outlandish wagon was all over town. By noon, nearly everyone who could walk had come by to look at it. Most had quite a bit to say to Sam, generally along the lines of, "Sam, you're crazier than we thought you were."

Some people got around to asking him, "And just where are you planning to go in that thing?"

"Denver," said Sam. "I've heard they've made silver strikes in the mountains up behind Denver. I figure the wind wagon would be the best way to get there."

"Denver's six hundred miles!"

"There's wind all the way," said Sam.

After that, Sam got hardly a minute's peace. Sociable as he was, he got pretty tired of admitting he might be crazy, but nevertheless, he was headed for Denver.

Not everybody thought the wind wagon was a joke. Joe decided to go with Sam. "I've taken a pretty good look at that wagon of yours," he said. "I don't see how you can manage the sail and that steering stick at the same time. I'll come along and give you a helping hand."

"That stick is called a tiller," said Sam. "And I'm glad you'll be coming along."

Mary Alice Bellows, a townswoman, said she would make the sail. "A blacksmith you may be, Sam Peppard, and a carpenter too. But I expect there are some things you can't do." she said.

12

Sam had been thinking about the master sailmakers he had seen back east. He knew they had a skill in their fingers that he didn't have. He accepted Mary Alice's offer. "I thank you kindly, Miz Bellows. I'll bring you a silver locket," he said to her.

One afternoon when Sam was getting ready to close up shop, he looked up and saw a thin gray man with a weather-beaten face watching him silently from the doorway. Sam had seen him a time or two before and knew that the old man farmed a claim to the west of Oskaloosa. "Howdy, oldtimer," Sam said.

The old man just stared at the wind wagon for a long moment. At last he spoke. "Thought you ought to know, my shack blew away."

"Too bad," said Sam.

"Cow, too."

Sam said nothing.

"Wind's mighty strong out there."

15

There was a long pause. "My wind wagon is made to go with the wind."

There was a longer pause. "There's 'go with,'" said the old man to Sam, "and then there's 'blown away'. Can't see there's much difference."

After that the old-timer would come and stand in the doorway every day or two, staring at the wind wagon and shaking his head. Sam ignored him as best he could. The wind wagon was almost ready to go, and he was busy getting his regular work finished up. As he worked, he stopped now and then to add a little touch to the wind wagon. He painted *Wind Wagon, Oskaloosa* on the back panel. He polished up the brass fittings of the mast. He greased the big iron wheels until they turned sweetly, without a murmur of complaint.

One day, Joe dropped by. "I've been thinking, Sam," he said. "The two of us aren't going to be enough. There's a lot to do—

managing the sail, steering, keeping a look-out for trouble, gathering buffalo chips so we can have a fire, cooking, shooting rabbits to eat. We'll be too tired to go looking for silver when we get to Denver."

"Who did you have in mind?" asked Sam.

"What about the Graham boys? They don't talk much, and I reckon they're pretty good shots. One of them plays the banjo, too."

Sam knew the Graham boys, all right. They were the two most up-and-coming sons of a large family that lived on the edge of town. Their names were Abraham and Isaiah, but no one ever remembered which was which. They both were tall and lanky and silent, so they were just called the Graham boys.

"I don't guess they'd have got themselves steady jobs," said Sam. "I'll talk to them about it."

When he did, the boys looked at each other and allowed as how they weren't too busy this time of year and they wouldn't mind setting their eyes on the Rocky Mountains. But they did have one question. "Is that fool wagon of yours going to get us there for sure?" asked the Graham boys.

"The wind wagon will get us there," said Sam. "I'm just waiting for the right kind of wind to come along."

Chapter 3

ALL THE WIND that spring seemed to come from the west. Sam almost got discouraged. "There's one thing the wind wagon can't do, Joe," he said one day. "It can't sail into the wind. If it's blowing from the northeast or the southwest, we can just angle the sail a little and zigzag across the prairie. But if it's blowing straight out of the west, there's not much we can do."

One Saturday, Sam decided he couldn't wait any longer. The wind was still from the west, but it was so fresh and so sweet as he stood in the street and let it blow around him that he locked up the shop and went to look for Joe and the Graham boys.

"We've got to try the wind wagon out today," Sam told them. "I swear I can smell the snow melting in the high mountains and the flowers blooming in the foothills. One of these days the wind will be just right, and we've got to be ready to go."

So they hauled the wind wagon, by hand, to a big high piece of ground just north of town. It was about as flat as any place around Oskaloosa, but it had a steep slope at its east end.

"Perfect," said Sam. "Folks think the prairie is flat as a pancake, but we will definitely have to handle a few hills."

It was a tight squeeze in the wind wagon when they were all on board. One of the Graham boys said, "Don't know where you expect me to stick a banjo." But then Joe hoisted the sail and they were off.

Sam felt the wind in his hair. There was nothing ahead of the wagon—no horse, no ox—just the grassy field which seemed to pull itself under the wagon wheels smooth as silk. Well, not exactly. The wagon lurched and bumped along, and the Graham boys hung on for their lives, their faces white with fear, as if they might fall into a raging sea instead of Old Man Hicks's pasture.

All Sam could feel was the wind pushing the wind wagon along. The wind was solid. It was strong. It could push them all the way to Denver.

Some movement against the trees caught Sam's eye. He turned away from the on-rushing pasture and saw the old man from the claim. He was watching the wind wagon with fierce eyes, and Sam wondered for a second whether the old man wanted them to blow away or whether he hoped they wouldn't.

Just then the land sloped downward sharply. The wind was under the wagon's body. It was ballooning the sail and lifting the wind wagon off the ground. It occurred to Sam that the wind might blow them all the way to the Missouri River.

Then they were beyond the crest of the hill. The wind slackened and the wheels touched the earth again and bumped to a stop. After a minute they all got out and looked at the wind wagon. It was fine—no cracks, no bends.

"Well," said Sam, "this wagon takes to the wind. Give us a high enough hill and we might just take off. But I'll put a little ballast in front to keep the bow down and we'll stay on the ground, I guarantee." The Graham boys looked relieved.

The next day Sam was painting over a few scratches on the wagon box when he looked up to see the old-timer standing in the door-

way to the smithy. "You'd better get that thing fixed so that it stays on the ground," he said. "The wind's about to change."

For a minute Sam couldn't think of anything to say, which was unusual for him. But he collected himself. "We're ready," he said. "We'll make it to Denver—and back. I'll bring you a silver dollar."

But the old man shook his head. "Just keep that wagon on the ground," he said. "The wind out there . . . ."

The old man shook his head again. And then he was gone.

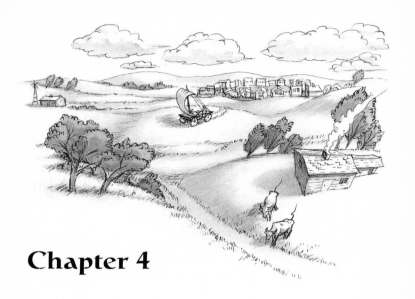

Chapter 4

THE WIND CHANGED the next day. It shift-
ed from west to southwest, just enough to
catch the wind wagon's sail and send them in
the right direction. Sam wasted no time. He
collected Joe and the Graham boys. They
packed up the sourdough and beans they had
ready, found a tight corner for the banjo and
a deck of cards, and sent out the word that
the wind wagon was ready to go.

Everyone in Oskaloosa showed up for the
great send-off, except for a couple of skeptics

who claimed Joe, Sam, and the Graham boys would be home by sundown, on foot. The old-timer didn't miss it. He stood at the back of the crowd, slowly shaking his head.

Sam paid him no attention. He stood up in the back of the wind wagon, waved his broad-brimmed hand, and said, "Folks, if you wanted to beat us to Denver, you should have started off three weeks ago." Then he sat down, set his hat squarely on his head to shade his eyes from the brilliant sun, and took hold of the tiller.

Joe pulled the sail around until the wind caught it, and several boys ran alongside the wagon to give it a push. And then the wind wagon, creaking a little, sailed off along the ridge road leading west out of town.

Three long days later they reached the edge of the Flint Hills where the land quits rolling and levels out into a five-hundred-mile slow upward incline to the Rocky Mountains. Before them lay the hard-packed road to

Denver, rutted and worn by the wheels of all the wagons that had carried people looking for land or gold or silver near Denver. In the distance they could see quite a swarm of prairie schooners lurching along.

"Come on, boys," said Sam Peppard, "we'll catch 'em before the sun is high!" He stretched his arms out as wide as he could and felt the strong prairie wind pulling at his shirtsleeves.

And so the great wind wagon voyage began. Sam had his accustomed place in the back of the wagon, handling the tiller. The others took turns looking after the sail and keeping lookout for buffalo or antelope or a fat prairie chicken to eat for dinner.

For the first week or so, the wind blew strong and steady. The wind wagon rolled along, overtaking wagons that moved slowly to the pace of a team of oxen. Sam loved to wait for the moment when people riding in those wagons heard the clatter of the wind

wagon and turned to stare in amazement at a wagon with a tall white sail and nothing pulling it. Then he would politely touch the brim of his hat as the wind wagon rattled past.

On the ninth day the wind died down. The folks in some of the slow, steady, ox-drawn wagons had the satisfaction of seeing the wind wagon drawn off the trail while its crew played cards and hunted rabbits. The people weren't very polite about it, either. "Never mind," said Sam. "They'll be eating our dust soon enough."

And Sam was right. When the wind blew again, it was fresher and stronger than ever. Sam, Joe, and the Graham boys soon pulled past the main body of wagons and had the road to themselves. For a good number of days the wind wagon rolled along so fast and so smoothly that even the Graham boys had to admit that it looked like they would live to see the Rocky Mountains.

On one of those days, Sam said, "I'd wager we're going twenty-five miles an hour." Since neither Joe nor the Graham boys had any notion about the wind wagon's speed— except knowing that they were going mighty fast—they didn't argue with Sam. But one of the Graham boys, who happened to have the side lookout spot, said, "Then I sure hope those Indians can't ride twenty-five miles an hour."

They all looked up and, sure enough, there were three Indians on spotted horses riding at a gallop in their direction. Now, Sam hoped he had never done anything to make any Indians sore at him, but he knew that a lot of Indians had a lot to be sore about, so he wasn't sure these Indians had friendly thoughts. And they were certainly coming on fast.

"Come on, wind wagon," he said, "now's the time to show what you can do." All the men hunkered down to give the sail a chance to do the most it could, while Sam fiddled with the tiller.

Joe lifted his head above the edge of the sideboards and said, "By gum, Sam, I think they're racing us."

Sam, Joe, and the Graham boys saw the Indians were riding about a hundred yards to the south of the wind wagon and about fifty yards back. Sam grinned. "Well, they've got themselves a race," he said.

The wind was with them that day. After about ten miles of hard riding, the Indians were getting closer but they were still behind the wind wagon. At last the Indians shouted something to each other, waved their arms in a friendly fashion, and turned south. That night, Sam went to sleep knowing that the wind wagon could surely go like the wind.

And the wind kept getting stronger and stronger as the land rose toward the Rockies. On some days they didn't raise the sail all the way up. "Either it will get blown to

35

rags, or that wind will take us right up into the air," said Sam. As he said it, he remembered the old-timer and thought, "It's just too bad that being blown away can't get you where you're going."

Chapter 5

ON THE MORNING of their twenty-second day on the road Sam studied the map while he drank his coffee. "I reckon we're just about eighty miles from Denver," he said. They were all feeling pretty good. Three weeks to Denver was mighty good time, especially considering the five or six days when they had done nothing but play cards and hunt rabbits.

Of course, the Graham boys were beginning to fret about the Rocky Mountains.

They could see the mountains already, looking like a solid cloud on the horizon. "They must be mighty high," one of the Graham boys said. "What if we fall off?"

Sam was a bit agitated himself as he got settled by the tiller, but he figured it was because he hated to come to the end of the wind wagon's first voyage.

He looked at the sky and thought they should have a good run. There were some dark clouds to the southwest, but the sky up ahead was clear blue and the wind had calmed down some. As the wagon picked up speed, Sam settled back and began to wonder how they were going to convince the people back in Oskaloosa that the wind wagon had really made it to Denver.

Suddenly an immense gust of wind hit the wind wagon broadside. The whole wagon shivered violently. At the same moment, Joe hollered, "It's a twister!"

Sam looked where Joe was pointing. Coming out of the southwest was a thin black finger of wind, twisting and snaking its way straight at the wind wagon, roaring like a thousand bulls spooked by thunder.

Sam gripped the tiller tightly. It seemed as if he should be able to dodge something so narrow. But the twister was coming fast. Sam knew if that fierce wind wanted the wind wagon, there was nothing he could do about it now.

"Lower the sail," he yelled. And then, "Jump, boys!" But there wasn't time for anything. The twister swirled down upon the wind wagon and lifted it straight up into the air, with Sam hanging onto the tiller and the others holding tight to anything they could grab a hold of.

Sam felt the huge force of the wind as it held the wagon and him and Joe and the Graham boys twenty feet above the prairie.

They hung in the air for so long Sam could have drawn a deep breath—if he had been thinking about breathing.

Then the twister dropped them, wind wagon and all, in a heap on the ground and went roaring away to the northeast.

It was a minute before Sam could see straight. The sudden silence felt strange to his ears, but he was all in one piece. He looked around at his crew. They didn't seem to be hurt. Joe was slowly shaking his head and the Graham boys were cautiously moving their arms and legs. But the wind wagon was in a thousand pieces.

Sam looked at the tangle of sail and the splintered boards and bent wheels. "Well, boys," he said, "it looks like we walk the rest of the way." He finally took a deep breath. "But it sure was some ride while it lasted."

As it turned out, one of the lumbering freight wagons came along. With a few smirks and rude jokes, the driver offered

41

them a ride into Denver. "Unless my team gets blowed away, of course," he said.

Sam just said, "Thank you kindly." But he remembered the power of that wind and knew that oxen could fly, too.

Joe found the back panel with the proud words *Wind Wagon, Oskaloosa* painted on it and handed it to Sam. It was hardly scratched. Sam put it under his arm. All the men climbed aboard the freight wagon and rode into Denver.

That's almost the end of the story. Sam, Joe, and the Graham boys did go silver mining before they hopped another wagon back to Oskaloosa. Sam brought home enough silver to build himself the little house and the lumber mill he'd been planning.

The old-timer showed up the day Sam stoked up the fire in his smithy. "You gonna build another of them wagons?" he asked. "Or have you had enough?"

"I'm not going to build another wind wagon," said Sam. "I'd never find a wind like I found the first time. I reckon I've gotten the most out of a wind wagon that I ever could. Some things are only meant to be done once. I'm going to settle down and stay put in Oskaloosa."

Sam did just that. He married, had ten children, and lived to be known for his long white beard. But he never forgot the wind wagon, especially when a strong wind blew from the southwest, bringing the smell of prairie grass and dust.

On such a day, Sam would gather his nearest grandchild to him and say, "Let me tell you a story about where that kind of wind took me. You might not believe it, but it's true. It's the story of the wind wagon. Just listen."

Author's Notes

After you read *The Wind Wagon* you might ask, "Is that a true story?"

Here is the answer: Sam Peppard was real, the wind wagon was real, and the tornado was real. But it all happened more than 100 years ago, so we can't ask Sam why he wanted to go on such a journey or how it felt to have his dream destroyed so suddenly. The story you read contains a lot of imagination and many facts that have been taken from other historical records. Here is some of the information that went into the telling of this story.

What the newspapers said

Kansas newspapers in the summer of 1860 reported that Sam Peppard of Oskaloosa had built a wind wagon and had sailed, with three other men, to within 80 miles of Denver. Unfortunately their trip had been cut short by a "whirlwind" that destroyed the wind wagon.

Articles from newspapers of the time contained different descriptions of the wind wagon. One account said the wind wagon was six inches deep, another said it was two feet deep! The newspapers did agree on the wagon's length and width and put the height of the mast at about ten feet.

What Sam Peppard said

Sam (who pronounced his last name like the word *peppered*) wrote an account of his journey. He said, "There were, you know, a great many people en route for the gold fields in those days. . . .Many amusing incidents happened and we had no little fun joking the teamsters as we flew by them." He told about the race with the Indians, too, and about the whirlwind. "In an instant the whirlwind struck the wagon and carried it about twenty feet into the air. When the wagon came down it struck on the hind wheels and they broke down under the weight. By what seemed a miracle, none of us was hurt."

Some of the people in Oskaloosa and in Sam's family remembered stories about the wind wagon and put their memories into writing. This helped to bring the story to life. But to understand why Sam build the wind wagon and how the journey might have felt, more research was needed.

Kansas in 1859 and 1860

Kansas was changing fast in these years. Before 1859 there had been fierce conflict between people who wanted Kansas to enter the Union as a slave state and those who wanted it to be a free state, not allowing slavery. But in 1859 a free-state constitution had been approved by the voters. Everyone knew that peace had come to

Kansas Territory and that it would soon be a state. Thousands of people decided to claim land in Kansas and become farmers or ranchers. Others, like Sam Peppard, came to build new towns.

Getting across the prairie

While many people wanted to settle in Kansas, many more were only interested in crossing the Kansas Territory, which stretched from the Missouri border to the crest of the Rocky Mountains. (The present boundaries of Kansas were set in 1861 when Kansas became a state.)

Some of these travelers wanted to get to the mountains of Colorado, where gold had been discovered at Pikes Peak in 1858. Others were headed for Oregon or for the goldfields of California.

So every year, thousands of people made the long trek across the prairie. The first

200 miles of Kansas Territory weren't bad. There was plenty of water and even some settlements where supplies could be bought and repairs made. But then came hundreds of miles of flat, empty prairie. Some people called it the Great American Desert because there was little water, no trees, and a lot of dust.

Horace Greeley was a famous newspaper editor. In 1859, he rode in a stagecoach along the same route as the wind wagon would take. He noticed the thickness of the grass and listed all the animals who lived in this land that people mistakenly called a desert.

Greeley saw herds of 10,000 or more buffalo at one time and many antelope. He also saw coyotes (which he called prairie wolves), gray wolves, prairie dogs, prairie chickens, rattlesnakes, blacksnakes, and burrowing owls.

Greeley knew that the Kansas Territory was not a desert. He said so in the letters he wrote to newspapers back east.

Why build a wind wagon?

The trek across Kansas Territory was hot, dusty, and grueling. A wagon train could take two or three months to get from the Missouri River to the Rocky Mountains and two or three more months to get to California or Oregon. Travelers wanted a faster, easier method, and many enterprising people thought of plans to make it happen.

A man named Rufus Parker planned to build a giant balloon, driven by propellers, that would take passengers from New York to San Francisco in three days. He tried to sell tickets to finance his project, but people didn't believe that it would work.

Some people started stagecoach lines. A fast horse-drawn stagecoach could travel from Independence, Missouri, to San Francisco, California in three weeks, but it was very expensive, especially since any household goods would have to be shipped separately. Ordinary people, especially families going west to claim land, couldn't afford the fare.

A plain wooden wagon, which anyone could build, pushed by the wind, which was free, was a logical—though risky—idea. And Sam Peppard wasn't the only one to think of it.

Several Kansans tried the wind wagon idea, but few were as successful as Sam. A man named John Parker used horses to take his wind wagon out on the level prairie near Westport, Kansas and left it there while he rested for the night. He had planned to take off for the West the next morning, but when he returned, he found only wheel tracks in the grass. He had left the sail up, and the wind had blown his wagon on a wild ride far out onto the prairie. He never found it.

Another Westport man, named Mr. Thompson, built the grandest wind wagon of all. It was 25 feet long and 7 feet wide, with space inside for cargo as well as passengers. Unfortunately, Thompson tried to show off the speed of his craft to investors. When he lost control, the wagon careened across the prairie and then crashed. So Sam Peppard and his crew did well to almost reach Denver.

In the end it was the railroad that made it easy to cross the prairie. By 1869, the transcontinental railroad was completed and prairie schooners stopped making their slow journeys across the plains.

Yes, there are tornadoes

It is true that there is a lot of wind on the prairies. It blows dust in a dry year and snow in a blizzard, and it fans the flames of a prairie fire. It also makes beautiful patterns in the waving grass and keeps the sky changing all the time.

The prevailing wind in Oskaloosa comes from the southwest. Sam would not often feel a wind straight from the east.

Sam mentioned that he had to keep the wagon to a speed that was safe for it. "Our best time was two miles in four minutes. We could not run faster than that rate or the boxing [axles] would have heated." If there was too much wind, Sam would simply "put on the brake and reef my sail."

Tornadoes are another matter. They aren't common anywhere, but the wind wagon sailed right through the territory that has the most tornadoes in the world. This is because cold, dry air from Canada bounces off the Rockies and meets warm, moist air from the Gulf of Mexico. The result of this combination is that the air currents begin to rotate and at times form the swirling, funnel-shaped windstorm that is a tornado.

Tornadoes are very powerful. Violent winds whirl around the center of these storms at speeds of more than 200 miles per hour. Most tornadoes measure less than one hundred yards in diameter but they can cause widespread death and destruction. Sam and his crew had seen several other whirlwinds during their journey. They were able to lower the sail, and the twisters passed a safe distance away. In the end the wind wagon adventurers were not so lucky, but they were not really unlucky, either. A tornado can take the roof off a house, suck the water out of a well, or toss a car in the air. Sam was right in proclaiming that it was a miracle that none of them was hurt.

Even in Tornado Alley, the area from Texas up through Kansas where most tornadoes occur, many people might never see a tornado. But they worry about them. Not long after Sam Peppard rode the whirlwind, an inventor decided to do something about the situation. He invented a "tornado killer"—it was a box full of dynamite that was set off when the wind reached tornado proportions. The explosion was supposed to blow the tornado apart. These boxes were set up along the southwest edge of a town, since most tornadoes came from that direction. Unfortunately it turned out that other things, like a crow brushing against the device, could set it off. People finally decided that all the explosions were more trouble than a tornado, which might never come, anyway.

Sam Peppard, the wind wagon, and the story

In the past an adventure like Sam's would be remembered by storytellers. It probably would become a legend. Some of the facts might get lost, but people would know that four men set off on a risky and exciting journey. They rode a whirlwind and lived to tell the tale.

Today, we like facts. We want to know what is true, and that is important, too. But if you want to tell the story of the wind wagon yourself, imagine it in your own mind and tell it in your own words. You will find, then, that the story has a life, a real life, of its own.